# Markova
## — REMEMBERS —

### DAME ALICIA MARKOVA DBE

Hamish Hamilton · London

Design by Craig Dodd

First published in Great Britain 1986
by Hamish Hamilton Ltd
27 Wrights Lane London W8 5TZ

**British Library Cataloguing in Publication Data**
Markova, Alicia
    Markova remembers.
    1. Markova, Alicia    2. Ballet dancers——Great
Britain——Biography
    I. Title
    792.8'092'4    GV1785.M3
    ISBN 0-241-11953-7

Typeset, printed and bound in Great Britain
by Butler & Tanner Ltd, Frome and London

# Acknowledgments

My thanks must go first of all to Craig Dodd, who has designed this book, and to Penelope Hoare of Hamish Hamilton, most helpful of editors.

The pictures in this book owe everything to their photographers, and to the most generous assistance of Miss Sarah Woodcock of the Theatre Museum, and of Mr Philip Dyer. Mrs Nesta MacDonald discovered some rare pictures for me with her customary skill. Miss Jane Pritchard of Ballet Rambert's archives; Miss Francesca Franchi of the Royal Opera House, Covent Garden archives; Mr William Poole of the Royal Academy of Dancing's Arnold Haskell collection; and the staff of the Dance Collection of the New York Public Library were also very helpful indeed in providing photographs. To my sister Doris Barry go all my thanks for her precious time and help given in searching for material in my own collection.

And last but not least I offer my sincere gratitude to Clement Crisp for encouraging me to record these memories.

A.M. London 1986

# CONTENTS

## Half-title photograph

MY SMALL HANDS AND FEET HAVE ALWAYS PRESENTED PROBLEMS with such basic matters as shoes and gloves—during one bitter winter when the Ballet Russe de Monte Carlo was touring and arrived in Chicago, I had to outfit myself with warm *Shirley Temple* gloves from the children's department of a big store, since nothing else would fit me.

There was a memorable moment, just after the war began in America, when we were dancing in San Francisco, and I needed new silk stockings. Next to the Saint Francis Hotel, where I was staying, was a shop where I had been told I would find the sort of stockings I always wore. When I told the assistant of my size, I was assured, in haughtiest tones, that "*nobody* has feet that small!" I was forced to reply that I did, indeed, have feet "that small", and could this elegant young lady say if there was a store in town where I might find some? "There isn't one," came the reply. "You need to use your feet. Take *more exercise* so they'll get larger, and then you'll find a size to fit you." This piece of sound advice reduced another member of the Ballet Russe, who was with me, to hysterical laughter. We left, stockingless.

# CHILDHOOD & THE DIAGHILEV YEARS 1910-29

# Childhood

IN THAT FAR-OFF CHILDHOOD BEFORE THE FIRST WORLD WAR, I remember being surrounded by colour and music.

My mother always said that I could, even as a baby, be left, perfectly happy if a vase of flowers was within my sight and music was playing in the background. These early delights of my infancy were combined with the excitements of the park. I was born in Finsbury, North London, and memories astonishingly are still clear of being taken in my pram to hear the band in Finsbury Park. There are the faintest echoes of marches which I must have learned to enjoy even then, for I love them still and associate them with dancing. (My early private lessons with George Balanchine, when I was a fourteen-year-old girl dancing with the Diaghilev Ballet, were shared with Alexandra Danilova, and Balanchine used to hum marches to accompany our work, since we did not have a pianist.) Another childhood memory is of the lake in Clissold Park, with its swans. This cannot have been a formative influence, but I can at least think of it as an omen for the future.

All these impressions are of the pre-war years, for I was born in 1910. My father, Arthus Marks, was a mining engineer. He was of the Jewish faith, with Polish ancestry some generations back. My mother, Eileen, was Irish, from County Cork, and this intermingling of races must account for some of my qualities as a little girl. In later life the mixture certainly helped me in working with the Russian Ballet: there is a temperamental similarity between Russians and Irish, laughing at one moment, crying the next.

I adored my father, and I was very close to him. He had hoped for a son as his first-born; instead, his family was eventually made up of four girls. When I came along he seems to have thought philosophically, "Oh, well. Never mind!" and decided to take me off to watch Arsenal playing football. At the age of two I can just remember being perched on my father's shoulders and encouraged to pipe, "Buck up, The Reds!" My mother was physically delicate, and a recurrent early image is of her resting in a hammock in our garden while I played alone. She was, I suppose, expecting the birth of one of my sisters. I was not quite four when Doris was born; then, after three more years, came Vivienne; and then Berenice (Bunny, the baby) arrived a year later.

I was a docile, even-tempered child, curious about life but silent, solemn-eyed and very frail. Because of childhood ill-health, my education was intermittent, and dancing lessons were begun in order to strengthen what were thought to be weak limbs. My little flat foot-prints were noted in the sands

*Previous page:* Le Rossignol: *London 1927. For the Prince's Theatre season I had to wear a chiffon tunic and pants rather than the white silk all-over tights that Matisse first designed.*

*Aged 3.*

at Bognor, where we were on holiday, and our doctor suggested that the exercise of classical ballet would strengthen my legs and feet. So I was sent to Saturday classes at the Thorne Academy, near our home in Muswell Hill. There I learned "fancy dancing" with a little barre work, waltzing, folk dance, and even the use of Indian Clubs swung to music. The school, though, was a serious one, and Miss Thorne approached my parents and insisted that I should have extra lessons, since she sensed that I might have some special ability. Soon I progressed to performing little solos in dance competitions, which seemed to me the most natural thing in the world. Then, as dancing began to mean more and more to me, I was taken to see Pavlova in a programme she gave at the Queen's Hall.

The effect was breath-taking. This was real dancing, and I knew that I had to try to talk to this glorious being. I pleaded with my father, and at the interval—and with a reluctance he did not let me see—he went back-stage and by some miracle persuaded Victor Dandré, Pavlova's husband, that I was a young dancer (he did not say *how* young!) who would count it an immense honour to see the great ballerina. "Not after the performance," came the reply. But the "young dancer" might present herself at Ivy House, Pavlova's home in Golder's Green, and be seen the next morning.

So it was that my father took me to see Pavlova the next day. Inside Ivy House there was an entrance hall littered with theatrical skips, for Pavlova was just about to start another tour. Suddenly she appeared, dressed in pale mauve. My father was left to read the morning papers while I was taken to her studio, where I changed, and was then put through my paces. Nothing more was asked of me. Pavlova watched me, corrected me, and gave me advice—not the least important being that I should always take very good care of my teeth, and always have a cologne rub after dancing. She rubbed me down herself with her cologne, and gave me the warning that there was only hard work ahead of me if I continued in the ballet.

My education was, because of a succession of childhood complaints—they included chicken pox, measles, whooping cough—sometimes sketchy. So school lessons were supplemented by "Guggy", Gladys Hogan, our nanny-cum-governess-cum-general helper. She encouraged me to read, helped my studies by teaching me, and became increasingly protective as the years went by and my professional career began.

This happened because, in December 1920, my father arranged for me to audition for the Kennington Theatre pantomime, which always used young dancers. Aged just ten, I was accepted as principal dancer for *Dick Whittington*, and was rewarded by my father with tea in a restaurant, much enhanced in my eyes by the magnificent cream cakes. I had to have a licence from the London County Council in order to appear, and for this I was examined by their doctor, and successfully passed the test of the school inspector, which suggests that my education at Guggy's hands was not without merit. I was granted a licence on the understanding that I would be chaperoned and tutored during the run of the pantomime. I was billed as *Little Alicia, The Child Pavlova*, and was paid the then princely sum of £10 per week to dance in two shows a day.

Thus I began my career, though without willing it. A dutiful child, I did what I was told, because I loved to dance. I let everyone else take the decisions. Guggy was with me at all times and, to make my first appearance at rehearsals, she dressed me in black velvet with ermine trimmings, in which I looked every inch the miniature ballerina! I danced three numbers in the pantomime, appearing as a poppy, then as a butterfly, and in an Oriental dance in the Sultan's Palace scene at whose climax I stood stock still, screamed, and fell flat on my back— a moment which always had a tremendous effect upon the audience. (The fall, incidentally, stayed with me throughout my career as the final collapse at the end of the mad-scene in *Giselle*.)

With my career thus launched, I was thereafter to earn my own living. Certain financial troubles were making themselves evident at home. My father was a brilliant and successful engineer, but unwise investment and even worse advice from

*In my first role as* Salome *in the pantomime* Dick Whittington, *in 1920.*

associates encroached on his income. My success in the pantomime, and the fact that my dancing had received serious notice in the newspapers, prompted a search for serious dance training.

Serafine Astafieva was the outstanding ballet teacher in London at this time. A former member of the Imperial Ballet in St Petersburg, a dancer in the early seasons of the Diaghilev Ballet, she came to London in 1916 and opened a school in the Kings Road, Chelsea, at what was known as The Pheasantry. I was thus taken to her studio by my mother, who announced our arrival with one of my professional cards which told of *Little Alicia, The Child Pavlova*. Astafieva flew into a towering rage and suggested we leave. There was no such thing as a Child Pavlova! Pavlova was a supreme artist! I wept. Tears melted Astafieva's heart—she was, as I discovered thereafter, the most generous and inspiring of women—and I was told that I should dance for her and her pupils at the end of their class. This I did. As I finished, Astafieva hugged me and told my mother, "I will accept her. Take her home. Wrap her in cotton wool—you have a race horse."

Thus I started to attend daily class with Astafieva, accompanied by the faithful Guggy. Throughout the spring and summer of 1921 I worked very hard. One morning the door of the studio opened and a very elegant gentleman came in, another man at his side. This was Serge Diaghilev, with Serge Grigoriev, his faithful lieutenant. Diaghilev was contemplating the great staging of *The Sleeping Princess* which he was to present at the Alhambra Theatre that autumn, and he was looking for extra dancers. Naturally he came to Astafieva's class in quest of talent, since they were good friends. I knew who Diaghilev was, for my parents had already taken me to see his company when the Ballet returned to London at the end of the war, and I can still see in my mind's eye the fantastic make-up worn by Lydia Sokolova as Kikimora in Massine's *Contes Russes*.

Diaghilev watched our class, indicated that a couple of students might be engaged for the forthcoming production. Among them was Patrick Healey-Kaye, just seventeen years old, already a most talented and promising dancer, and eventually to be renamed Anton Dolin. He was my *bête noire*, for he used to pinch me and pull my hair in class, so that I always tried to get as far away as possible from him during barre work. Diaghilev then pointed to me, very amused, asking about this "little one". I was asked to dance, and I performed a solo to the Rubinstein *Valse Caprice*. As I finished, there were murmurings with Astafieva. Diaghilev called me to him, kissed me, and left.

Next morning in class I was told that Diaghilev wished to include me in *The Sleeping Princess* as the Fairy Dewdrop, smallest of the fairies in the Prologue, with a new variation choreographed for me by Bronislava Nijinska. Despite the fact that the LCC licencing age for minors had been raised to twelve years, and I was just ten years and eight months, Diaghilev somehow persuaded the authorities that I was very special, and that my solo would only last two minutes in the Prologue. I was granted permission to appear, a fact which I promptly celebrated by developing diphtheria. I was whisked off to the isolation hospital where I spent agonising and depressing weeks. A form of rescue came when I was out of quarantine, for Diaghilev arranged that tickets should be made available for Guggy and me to go to performances of the ballet, and thus I saw this incomparable staging with each of its superlative ballerinas as Aurora. Sometimes I sat with Diaghilev.

As a consolation Diaghilev also promised me that if I worked hard he would consider me for his company when I was grown-up. I now had something to aim for, a real and clear purpose of my own.

I continued to study earnestly with Astafieva, appearing occasionally in her school displays and in charity performances. Just after my twelfth birthday, I obtained my next professional engagement. Nicholas Legat had been one of the greatest *danseurs* and teachers at the Mariinsky Theatre in St Petersburg. Now in his fifty-third year he, with his wife Nadine Nikolayeva Legat, had an engagement with a group known as the Russian Art Dancers at the London Palladium, as part of a Music Hall bill. Inevitably, Legat came to Astafieva's to recruit dancers, and Pat Dolin was among those chosen. I was also selected, in order to dance a version of Pavlova's *Dragonfly* solo, arranged by Legat. The season was very hard work—we played twice nightly, and three times on matinee days—but successful. The year that followed was a continuation of hard work with Astafieva, at charity performances and at auditions. But then came the tragic death of my father.

I was shattered by this, for Father had been very close to me and, furthermore, our family finances were hard hit. Obviously I should try and earn in the theatre, but there seemed little likelihood of work. Pat Dolin wrote often from the Diaghilev company, with whom he was now dancing, with messages that Diaghilev had enquired how "the little one" was progressing. Pat evidently reported back on my studies, for one afternoon

I was summoned by Astafieva back to her studio. I had been lunching with Mrs Haskell, Arnold Haskell's mother, a friend of Astafieva who often watched our classes. The telephone rang: Astafieva, demanding that I hasten back to The Pheasantry to dance for Diaghilev who was also bringing Bronislava Nijinska with him.

I had just eaten a hearty lunch, but I raced to the studio and auditioned for Madame Nijinska for two hours. As a result, I learned that I was to be considered as a member of the Ballet Russe in the New Year of 1925, and that Guggy and I would be able to live with the Nijinska family, which included her young daughter, and that they would be able to keep an eye on us.

There ensued one of those convulsions which periodically affected the Diaghilev company. Madame Nijinska left suddenly. She was succeeded as company choreographer by George Balanchine, lately arrived in the West from Petrograd (Leningrad). Once more, while visiting Mrs Haskell, I was summoned to Astafieva's studio because Diaghilev wanted to see me dance again, this time in company with Balanchine.

Balanchine gave me an exhaustive audition in which I danced everything I knew, and Pat Dolin partnered me in some *pas de deux* I had learned. Balanchine seemed determined to push me as far as he could, and it was then that he discovered that I was able to perform double *tours en l'air* (which is a step usually performed by men) and multiple *fouettés*, as well as acrobatic movement. He needed these skills because, though I did not know it at the time, he was about to re-choreograph Stravinsky's *Le Rossignol* for Diaghilev. The final decision rested with Balanchine. He chose me to dance the role of the Nightingale. The die was cast. I was to join the Ballet Russe as the first "baby ballerina".

*August 1911. With my father, grandfather and great-grandfather.*

*With my mother on my second birthday.*

*At Margate, with my mother and my sister Doris. Aged 5.*

*Opposite: My L.C.C. Licence to dance at the Royal Albert Hall, aged 12. The cap I am wearing was made of silver lace.*

*The Sylvia pizzicato. Aged 11.*

# LONDON COUNTY COUNCIL.

## EDUCATION OFFICER'S DEPARTMENT.

## LICENCE.

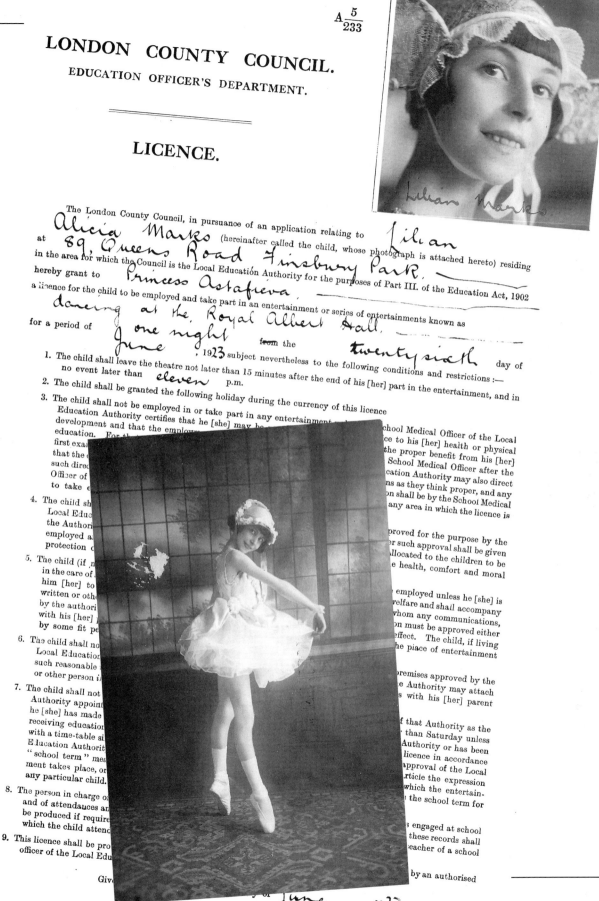

The London County Council, in pursuance of an application relating to *Alicia Marks* (hereinafter called the child, whose photograph is attached hereto) residing at *89, Queens Road Finsbury Park.* in the area for which the Council is the Local Education Authority for the purposes of Part III. of the Education Act, 1902 hereby grant to *Princess Astafieva,* a licence for the child to be employed and take part in an entertainment or series of entertainments known as *dancing at the Royal Albert Hall,* for a period of *one night* from the *twentysixth* day of *June*, 19*23* subject nevertheless to the following conditions and restrictions :—

1. The child shall leave the theatre not later than 15 minutes after the end of his [her] part in the entertainment, and in no event later than *eleven* p.m.

2. The child shall be granted the following holiday during the currency of this licence

3. The child shall not be employed in or take part in any entertainment... School Medical Officer of the Local Education Authority certifies that he [she] may be... development and that the employ... education. For th... first exa... that the... such direc... Officer of... to take...

4. The child sh... Local Educ... the Authori... employed a... protection...

5. The child (if... in the care of... him [her] to... written or oth... by the authori... with his [her]... by some fit pe...

6. The child shall no... Local Education... such reasonable... or other person i...

7. The child shall not... Authority appoint... he [she] has made... receiving education... with a time-table si... Education Authorit... "school term" mea... ment takes place, or... any particular child.

8. The person in charge o... and of attendances an... be produced if require... which the child attend...

9. This licence shall be pro... officer of the Local Edu...

Giv... *June*, 1923

*Princess Astafieva rehearsing us in her
studio, with my governess, Guggy,
sitting on the piano stool, watching me
closely. 1922.*

# With Diaghilev

ON THE FIRST DAY OF JANUARY 1925, JUST ONE MONTH AFTER MY fourteenth birthday, I became a member of the great Diaghilev Ballet.

My mother had to stay in England with my three younger sisters, and so I was accompanied on the journey to join the company by Guggy, who was my governess and chaperone. My salary was £2. 10s per week. We left London on a morning of thick fog, and amid the bustle of Victoria Station I met Ninette de Valois for the first time. She was to shepherd Guggy and me to Paris and thence to Monte Carlo – I recall how impressed we were by her beautiful French, and by her elegance.

Almost before I could collect my thoughts, I was engulfed in the daily life of the Ballet Russe. Looking back now, I marvel at the child I was, and the life I was to lead. To anyone else it might have seemed totally artificial, but to me it was all I knew, and I was content to let every decision be taken for me. Diaghilev, present or absent, dominated my life. Physically he seemed to me a huge man: he would stand on stage before a performance, his coat slung over his shoulders, his back to the lowered curtain, a cane in his hand and Grigoriev or Kochno by his side. We would be warming up, and he might ask me how I was and kiss me on the forehead. Emotionally he became a father-figure to me: the fact of his gentleness to me, calling me his "new daughter" or *dushka* (little darling), seemed natural. I hardly ever spoke, and I think he loved that, and also my complete innocence. The innocence was preserved by the company through my five years with the Ballet Russe, and in a sense I suppose it rather isolated me, because I was so much younger than any of the other dancers except Lifar, who was already marked out as Diaghilev's protégé. Of course, Pat Dolin and Ninette de Valois, while they were there, were affectionate and helpful; and my first mentor was Lydia Sokolova (the Englishwoman Hilda Munnings, entirely Russian in outlook and artistry). But it was Alexandra Danilova who became like an elder sister to me, because she spoke a little English, and she was then, as she remains to this day, one of my dearest friends.

Some members of the company were frightened of Diaghilev. None, not even Serge Grigoriev, our *régisseur* and Diaghilev's closest practical associate, understood why he should be so interested in me. Diaghilev worried about my education and arranged for me to have French lessons as soon as I arrived. He insisted that I grow my hair from its "Buster Brown" cut to something longer and more classical.

*My first appearance in London as "Markova" with the Diaghilev Ballet at the Coliseum in 1925.*

He took me to visit museums and told me to listen to music.

Special costumes had to be made for me because of my minute size, though I danced my first *Swan Lake* adagio in an altered tutu worn by Vera Trefilova, and felt honoured that I should wear a costume belonging to this illustrious prima ballerina.

The daily life of the company began with class at 9 a.m. Madame Cecchetti taught the corps de ballet, while the soloists and principals went to Maestro Cecchetti. Early in 1925, Maestro came to watch the end of his wife's class and noticed me working industriously, learning his method. Next day I was told by Grigoriev that I must thenceforth attend Maestro's class—a rare privilege—and later, during a week when I had no performance with the company, which was away in Marseille, Maestro decided to give me class every morning with his private pupils, amongst whom were Ruth Page, Vincenzo Celli and Chester Hale. Instead of the customary sixty minutes, we were treated to three-hour sessions. I realized what a priceless gift I was being given, but at the end of three hours—with Maestro seeming to have no idea of time, and intent upon setting me a variation to dance—I was exhausted. As the week progressed I had to murmur that three hours of such concentrated teaching was all my very slight frame could take, and when the company returned from Marseille I was very tired, though much stronger technically.

My first real challenge with the company came with *Le Rossignol*, for which I had been selected in London and which was being prepared during the spring of 1925. This was a new version by George Balanchine to replace the earlier Massine production which had been forgotten. It was also Balanchine's real début with the company as choreographer; his first creation in the West was also my first with the Ballet Russe. As rehearsals began, Balanchine tested me, thinking up steps which he supposed might be beyond me. Yet I managed to produce what he wanted, including a diagonal of *fouettés* across the stage and back, with arm movements as if swimming, which he felt gave the impression of a little bird hopping. In the *pas de deux* with Death (a role taken by Lydia Sokolova) I had to perform double *tours en l'air*. We rehearsed the solo off point, then one morning Balanchine asked me to dance it on point, which I obediently did. (Throughout my career I have always felt that if a choreographer asks for something, my attitude must always be, "Well, let's try." As a result I always had wonderful roles, and have usually managed to produce what the choreographer wanted. This lesson I learned early with Balanchine during

Le Rossignol, *London 1927*.

*Rossignol* rehearsals.) The result delighted Balanchine: it gave an uncanny effect to the choreography and accentuated my fragile appearance.

Because the original costume for the Nightingale—made for Karsavina—was unsuitable for me, I was taken to Paris to the apartment of Vera Soudeikina (who later married Stravinsky) since she was to make my new costume. Instead of the uninteresting brown nightingale outfit I had anticipated, I was clad in all-over white silk tights with diamond bracelets on arms and ankles, and Matisse, who was the designer for *Rossignol*, insisted that my hair be tucked into a white bonnet decorated with osprey feathers. During the fittings, Diaghilev, Matisse, Stravinsky and Kochno watched, while I stood mute, and they argued about osprey feathers. Diaghilev declared that they were exorbitantly expensive. Matisse—and Stravinsky—were determined that they should be used (this I gathered from the mixed Russian and French of their argument) and finally Matisse and Stravinsky agreed to share the cost. For many years afterwards Stravinsky, who was always paternal to me, called me *petichka* (little bird), and during the rehearsals of *Rossignol* he was kind and helpful, telling me not to be afraid of the music. His advice—the best advice possible—was, "Just listen. And *don't* count!"

Diaghilev, incidentally, did buy me feathers. Some years later, when the company was dancing in Manchester, I was rehearsing the Bluebird *pas de deux* on the Monday morning, for my first performance in it that evening. At that time the girl's head-dress was made of ostrich feathers and pearls, and Diaghilev declared this was too vulgar for me. He would like me to wear blue bird of paradise feathers and diamonds! But where would one get blue bird of paradise feathers in Manchester on a Monday morning? Diaghilev's reply was to produce two £5 notes from his pocket and give them to my mother with the instruction, "Go. Shop." By great good fortune she found feathers, and I have kept the head-dress to this day as a reminder of an improbable Monday in Manchester and of Diaghilev's taste and his concern. The diamonds are paste. But the bird of paradise feathers are real.

For my first two years in the company I was looked after—I could as well say guarded—by Guggy, who did everything for me. She supervised my life, my lessons, even dressing me in the theatre for performance, and she locked me up in our hotel room if she went out, so that no accident should befall me. (I remember once, when Alexandra Danilova came to take me out to tea, that I had to explain through the locked door that I couldn't get out until Guggy returned from the Post Office.) I was working diligently with the company, travelling across Europe, dancing in the greatest theatres. If I was not called for rehearsal my real pleasure was to spend afternoons in the darkened stalls of a theatre, seeing Diaghilev arrange the lighting for a ballet or listening to orchestral rehearsals. But Guggy, I now realize, had an almost pathological desire to isolate and protect me from the company. Eventually illness intervened, and she fell victim to heart disease and her phobias, dying insane. When her illness began I was effectively alone, looking after her. Diaghilev insisted that I rejoin the company in Paris, and I was placed in the care of Ninette de Valois. Ninette started to teach me how to look after myself, showing me how to order meals in restaurants, how to shop, how to cope. Later, when my mother was able to come out to take charge of me, the roles were reversed. My mother was gentle, charming, but unused to dealing with life abroad.

In many matters I found myself in charge, organizing meals, arranging our life on tour. I learned how to figure things out on our extended, but anything but glamorous, journeyings round Europe. The company travelled second class, eight to a compartment, sitting up and trying to sleep if we could. When we arrived at a new city where we were to perform, we grouped four or six dancers together, and a couple of the men in the group would go in search of lodgings. There were two Polish character dancers, the Hoyer brothers, who formed a group with Natalia Branitzka (who was married to Jan Hoyer), Vera Savina (the English Vera Clarke, who had been Massine's first wife), my mother and me. Arrived at a station, the Hoyer brothers would race off to find the best and cheapest lodgings while I was left perched on top of the cases like a waif until they returned and we could install ourselves in our temporary home.

For two years I had been billed as *Alicia Markova*, with a small repertory of soloist roles. At about the time when mother joined me, Diaghilev demoted me. I became just *Markova*, a member of the corps de ballet. I was sixteen, and Diaghilev knew that I had to develop from a child prodigy into a more mature artist. He explained to me that I must learn the hard way, and that it would be valuable to me later. I have blessed his decision ever since. I learned the repertory as a member of the corps de ballet, as a soloist, then as a ballerina, and this has helped my understanding enormously.

Gradually I started to win back my soloist roles, and gain others, but I was not a "young woman" in the accepted sense

*Monte Carlo, 1925. My very first* Swan Lake, *wearing Trefilova's costume. I was coached for the role by Mathilde Kschessinskaya.*
Inset. *At the battle of flowers in Monte Carlo in 1925, with Arnold Haskell and my governess, Guggy.*

*Wearing Arnold Haskell's cap and gown at Cambridge, 1922.*

*Now I have earned my own cap and gown. Receiving an honorary Doctorate of Music at Leicester University, from the Chancellor, Lord Adrian, in 1966.*

of the word. I was still delicate, and in many ways even more sheltered, despite the sophisticated surroundings of the Ballet Russe, than people imagined. I was still protected within the company. I worked unceasingly, learned all I could, and was sustained at every moment by my devotion to Diaghilev and what I knew was his real affection for me.

Because of my youth I was not permitted, by Diaghilev or Grigoriev (who was responsible for the day-to-day running of the company), to accept any of the invitations which came to the adult members of the company, or even to take presents from admirers. Lord Rothermere sent me a huge box of chocolates—he knew of my addiction to them—but they had to be returned. Only Chaliapine, who adored the company, was allowed to send me chocolates which I could eat.

I celebrated my eighteenth birthday in December 1928. We were in Monte Carlo and, as usually happened, members of the company were invited to dance brief numbers on a small stage specially placed in the ballroom of the Hôtel de Paris. At a charity gala, I danced the *pas de deux* from *Cimarosiana* with Serge Lifar. Massine had made very complex choreography, which I enjoyed. Diaghilev liked both of us in it, telling me that the costume by Jose-Maria Sert suited me.

After we had danced, I went to my dressing-room and prepared to go home. At this moment, Grigoriev appeared and said that Diaghilev wished to see me at his table in the ballroom. I was wearing only day clothes, but Grigoriev assured me that this did not matter. When I reached his table, Diaghilev told me that I had done very well. He asked me how old I was and, when I assured him that I was just eighteen, he said that I must have a glass of champagne for the first time in my life. The other people at the table—Lifar, looking very elegant in a dinner jacket, Tchernicheva, Danilova and Balanchine—declared that this must be my official "coming-of-age party". Diaghilev laughed, and I was thenceforth "of age". This meant that during the last summer of the company's existence, throughout the London season at Covent Garden, whenever invitations came for members of the company to go to receptions, I was allowed to attend. Arnold Haskell's mother—both she and Arnold had been dear and generous friends since my days as a student with Astafieva—bought me my first evening dress from Lanvin and, in my first really high-heeled shoes (of silver kid), I thought I was absolutely and definitely IT, as I went to my first grand party at Lady St Just's house in Cavendish Square.

But I must have seemed a conundrum to the outside world.

*Michel Georges Michel came back-stage to our dressing-room to draw me during the Paris Season of the Diaghilev Ballet at Christmas 1927. I had just danced* La Chatte, *but by the time he arrived, I was dressed and made-up for one of the Indian Girls in* Firebird.

*On holiday in August 1929: a photograph taken before the news of Diaghilev's death.*

I knew great theatres, applause, the beginnings of international fame (though it was other people, sometimes Diaghilev, who told me of critical appreciation of my work). I knew Stravinsky and Matisse as other girls of my age might know the music or art teacher at school. I knew the harsh reality of sitting upright all night in cramped second class railway carriages travelling through Belgium, France, Germany, Spain, Italy, Hungary, Austria, Czechoslovakia. I accepted this as part of the natural order of things. I was excited as the 1928/9 season ended, because Diaghilev had told me that for the forthcoming year I was to be a principal of the company, with roles planned for me, and that after five years of soloist and corps de ballet ranking, I could earn a ballerina's salary. I knew, too, that *Giselle* was to be revived for the great Olga Spessivtseva, and that I was to learn the role and dance it. The future was more than rosy.

After the summer season at Covent Garden, and a brief series of performances at Vichy, the company dispersed for the holidays, and I returned to England, to spend some time with friends at Littlehampton. I relaxed, pottering through idle days, thinking of nothing, occasionally aware that the next season would be very exciting. The newspapers, which I hardly glanced at, were delivered morning and evening. On 19 August 1929, the afternoon delivery came, and as I picked up the paper, a headline struck me like a fierce blow. DIAGHILEV DEAD.

For the first two weeks after the news, when I returned to London and to the two rooms my mother, my sisters and I occupied, I was in a state of shock. A letter from Grigoriev in Monte Carlo announced that the Diaghilev Ballet had come to an end. I felt that, at the age of eighteen, my life had come to an end, too. I became ill, because I could see no future for myself. I was a young woman possessed of a talent of the most special kind, which could only be used in the rarified world of the Ballet Russe. I was a stranger in England, for my real country was the Diaghilev company, and death had over-run it and I could never go back there. No wonder I felt sick. No wonder I could not dance, nor had the least inclination to do so.

The autumn and winter of 1929 passed in a kind of waking nightmare, for I lacked any energy or hope. Then Grigoriev announced in a letter that there would be a winter season of operas with ballets in Monte Carlo and that there was a place for me. At last I felt needed. Alas, the season was of little interest, and the only thing I recall with any pleasure is a *pas de trois* with Danilova and Tchernichova in *A Night in Venice*, in which Petroff, the choreographer, had given me a very difficult and brilliant variation. By March the season was over. The dancers dispersed again to find work where they could, and I returned to London with my mother, more distressed than ever.

My mother insisted that I occupy my time somehow, for there was no work for me since I was not a pretty blonde suited to musical comedy or revue. So I set myself to learn cooking and dress-making, and I was soon expert enough to make myself a very fashionable frock to wear at a garden party given by Heinemann, the publishers for whom Arnold Haskell was now working. Later, I was able to make my own costumes whenever this was necessary.

Then one day there came a letter. It was from a young man signing himself Fred Ashton, wondering if I would be interested in dancing with him.

*Class with Maestro Cecchetti, Monte Carlo, 1925; from left to right: Mme Cecchetti; Doubrovska; Markova; Majerska; Nina Nikitina; Geva; Klemetska; Komarova; Sokolova; Unger; Troussevich; Chamié; Lapitsky; Lifar; Tcherkas; Alice Nikitina; Dolin; Danilova; Zalevska; Savina; Maestro Cecchetti.*

Carnaval *in London with the Diaghilev Ballet in the winter season at the Coliseum, 1925. I am dancing* Papillon, *with Nicholas Legat as Pantalon and Jean Jazvinsky as Pierrot.*

La Chatte *with the Diaghilev Ballet in 1927.*

*In Monte Carlo with my mother, 1926.*

*The Diaghilev Ballet, mid-channel between Newhaven and Dieppe, 1926. I am seated in front of Ninette de Valois, in her care.*

Aurora's Wedding *with the Diaghilev Ballet at the London Coliseum in 1925. Nicholas Kremnev; Tatiana Chamié; myself, as Little Red Riding Hood; Louba Soumarokova; and our régisseur, Serge Grigoriev. Chamié and Soumarokova were the two Porcelain Princesses, Kremnev the Mandarin, in Nijinska's interpolated Chinese Dance.*

*On tour in Edinburgh with the Diaghilev Ballet in 1928. From left to right: Albert King, the company manager for England; Leon Woidzikovski; Alexandrina Troussevich; Serge Lifar; Felia Doubrovska, with behind her our conductor, Roger Desormière; Alexandra Danilova; George Balanchine; Lyubov Tchernichova; myself and my mother.*

# THE BIRTH OF BRITISH BALLET 1930-38

FRED ASHTON'S LETTER WAS A BOLT FROM THE BLUE. I DID NOT
know him, but he wrote that he was to provide the dances for
a production of Dryden's *Mariage à la mode* which Sir Nigel
Playfair was to present at the Lyric Theatre, Hammersmith.
He had seen me dance with the Diaghilev Ballet and now he
asked if I would consider appearing with him. We arranged to
meet at the Hammersmith tube station, and he took me across
the road into Sir Nigel's office. I was invited to appear with
Fred, with four other dancers to support us (they included
Walter Gore), and my admiration for Fred increased when he
insisted that I be paid a proper fee of £10 per week. Once into
rehearsals, it was obvious that young Mr Ashton was vastly
talented. The production, which starred Athene Seyler, Angela
Baddeley and Glen Byam Shaw, was a success, and in time we
transferred to the Royalty Theatre in Soho.

This seems to me the time when British ballet was born. At
this moment the Rambert company, the Vic-Wells Ballet and
the Camargo Society were all starting up. I was able to participate in the work of all three. I appeared in a new production
each month, joining in the experiments as well as dancing the
classic repertoire. My abilities were at last to be used to help
the ballet in my own country.

Marie Rambert was making the real start of her company in
the Ballet Club performances which took place on Sunday
nights in her husband Ashley Dukes' Mercury Theatre
in Notting Hill Gate. Fred Ashton had been her earliest
choreographic discovery, and it was he who suggested to
Mim Rambert that I be asked to join the Ballet Club as guest
ballerina. And thus it was that Fred choreographed a version
of Dukas' *poème dansée*, *La Péri*, for me in the first Ballet Club
evening. Its Persian theme inevitably took us to Burlington
House, where there was a great exhibition of Persian Art, and
Fred, Billy Chappell—also a Rambert dancer—and I were able
to glean ideas about make-up, as well as about physical poses.
So, in the ballet, Fred and I drew our eyebrows in straight
lines across our foreheads, and I was able to indulge in purple
nail-varnish.

There was, needless to say, no money for the production.
Mim Rambert declared that everyone would receive 6s 6d per
performance, but I had to tell her that this would just pay for
the new shoes I needed for each performance and, as the curtain
was due to fall after the last bus to my home had departed, a
taxi would cost me an extra 4s. I could not afford to lose money
by appearing, and Mim agreed that both Fred and I should be
paid a stellar 10s 6d. Such were the stringencies of the times.

# Building British Ballet 1930-32

*Opposite: In 1930 Arnold Haskell
compiled and gave me this brochure to
send out to managements.*

*Previous page: As Nicolette, with the
Markova–Dolin Ballet, 1935.*

The production costs for *La Péri* were minimal. Billy Chappell had ingenuity as well as talent—he was able to make and design costumes as well as dance—and he created a beautiful tunic for Fred, who was the hero, Iskender, from a discarded brocade evening dress belonging to Mim (she hated parting with it!). I was flattered, but a bit aghast, since my costumes were to be made from new materials.

ALICIA MARKOVA

In her creation THE NIGHTINGALE
(Stravinsky's "Song of the Nightingale").

ALICIA MARKOVA

ALICIA MARKOVA joined the Russian Ballet in 1924, at the age of 14. She was the youngest dancer ever engaged by Serge Diaghileff, and most certainly the youngest dancer ever to appear in leading rôles.

Amongst her greatest successes are rôles created by such celebrated dancers as Karsavina, Kyasht, and Lopokova.

### RÔLES

The Cat in "THE CAT" (with Serge Lifar).

The Blue Bird in "AURORA'S WEDDING" (with Anton Dolin).

Pas de Deux in "CIMAROSIANA" (with Serge Lifar and Anton Dolin).
(The Rôle originally created by Karsavina)

Butterfly in "CARNIVAL."

Adagio in "THE SWAN LAKE."
(Monte Carlo 1925, at the age of 14).

Pas de Trois in "THE SWAN LAKE."

### CREATION

The Nightingale in Stravinsky's "SONG OF THE NIGHTINGALE."

— 2 —

" ALICIA MARKO..
won her praise wherever sh...
—*The Dancing* ..

. . .

" Last year a child prodigy, now a developed star."
—*The Dance*—August, 1929.

. . .

" A lovely bit of dancing by ALICIA MARKOVA, as the frail and beautiful nightingale. It stood out like a finely chiselled cameo."
—*The Dance*, New York—September, 1929.

. . .

" . . . her miming compared very favourably with that of the others, and her technique was *considerably superior*."
—*The Dancing Times*—August, 1929.

. . .

" ALICIA MARKOVA is brilliant in the rôle of the Nightingale . . . she is able to overcome the innumerable technical difficulties without any apparent effort."
Arnold L. Haskell in *Some Studies in Ballet.*

— 5 —

PRESS EXTRACTS

".. MARKOVA is a poem in her fragile candour and h.. nious movement."—*Continental Daily Mail*, June 18th, 1929

" A miniature duet between Death (Mme. Sokolova) and th.. Nightingale (Mlle. MARKOVA) was nothing short of marvellou.. brilliance."
—*Daily Mail*, July 19th, 19..

"CIMAROSIANA."

"There was about her a grace, an almost classic elegance, which was infinitely charming, and suggested future possibilities of great brilliance. She has something of that delicate fantasy in her appearance which is an essential attribute in a dancer of the first rank."—*The Graphic*, August 6th, 1927.

— 3 —

An Interview with Serge Diaghileff

"Watch the dancing of my English girl, ALICIA MARKOVA. Her promise is remarkable."
—*Manchester Evening News*—Nov., 1928.

"THE CAT."

"M. Diaghileff, the *Daily Dispatch* was informed last night, intends to make a prima ballerina of the English girl, ALICIA MARKOVA."
—*Manchester Dispatch*—Nov., 1928.

— 4 —

These first Sunday night shows at the Mercury were magical. I suppose that the theatre's postage stamp stage (all of eighteen feet square) should have surprised me after the vastness of La Scala, Milan, or the Paris Opéra, where we had danced with Diaghilev, but the Rambert enterprise was eager, young, full of happiness and enthusiasm at making ballets, and true artistry was the over-riding principle, and made us ignore shortage of space and shortage of funds.

The bare covering of my expenses for a Sunday evening performance was absolutely the way to the poor-house for me. I had to find work. Through Fred Ashton's good offices I was to appear in a cinema. At that time the Regal, Marble Arch, produced stage shows between the showings of films, and Fred was engaged to stage a ballet during the run of *Outward Bound*. So, three times a day, I made my descent on to the stage from a crescent moon in the Dance of the Hours from Ponchielli's *La Gioconda*, with Billy Chappell as my partner and an attendant corps de ballet of thirty-two girls. For my eighteen performances a week I received a proper commercial fee, and as I spun and pirouetted, I tried not to think of what I had so recently been accustomed to, with Diaghilev.

The show was successful, and the management asked me to stay on. At my request Fred continued to provide the choreography. His wonderful talent meant that the numbers were satisfying to dance, even in the scene where I found myself as the fox (in all-over brown leotard, large bushy tail, a bonnet with little ears and paw-like gloves) in a hunting divertissement, determinedly pursued by the corps de ballet as hounds. I had to flee the pack by spinning as fast as possible across the stage, and this—interspersed with acrobatic tricks and falls on to one knee—meant that within a couple of performances I was covered with bruises. My sister Doris, who helped look after me back-stage, spent much of her time running to a nearby chemist to buy witch-hazel and bandages to enable me—by now black and blue on knees and arms—to cope with the ardours of the chase.

Fred also produced a ravishing scene to the ballet-music from Gounod's *Faust*, the stage decorated all in white and the corps de ballet rising from the bowels of the cinema in long white tutus into this white setting, where I danced, in a classical tutu, a variation which I remember to this day—not only because it unfailingly brought the house down, but because of its brilliance and charm.

At this time the Camargo Society was also presenting evenings of ballet. Founded by Arnold Haskell and Philip

*Water Lily, a solo arranged by Dolin to Liszt's Third Consolation. Markova–Dolin Ballet, 1935.*

Richardson, it helped fill the gap left by the disappearance of the Diaghilev Company, giving subscription performances several times a year in order to find and encourage new talent. In 1931 Fred was to make a new work for a season which was to involve everyone in the young British ballet, irrespective of their allegiances. *Façade* used the music William Walton had composed to accompany Edith Sitwell's poems. I was given the *Polka*, which incorporated certain jokes between Fred and me. It was inspired by the Music Hall dancing of the time and included the "fall-over" step. The initial joke was that the audience should see me apparently posed at the back of the set, behind double doors, standing on point in a fetching skirt and wearing a boater. As I prepared to dance, my skirt dropped off, I stepped out of it and performed in bloomers, finishing with a double *tour en l'air*. On the first night the audience was initially amazed, then suddenly understood the joke, and roared; and subsequently, as the *Polka* usually stopped the show, I grew accustomed to repeating it.

The role of the Débutante in *Façade* was created by Lydia Lopokova, an adorable and witty dancer, but when *Façade* was taken into the repertory of the Ballet Club, I was asked to take over the part with its hilarious *Tango*. My interpretation was very different from Lopokova's, for my Débutante was a country bumpkin trying to be sophisticated. The original costume was, in any case, far from *soignée*. The Débutante wore a calf-length orange tutu and a little pink jacket made from cheap cotton satin which purposely fitted where it touched; high-heeled black tango shoes; black lace mittens; a Dolly Varden hat with red and orange flowers, topped by a very tired orange marabou tippet (rather like Nellie Wallace's "Little bit of vermin"). In the *Tango* she had to try and follow Fred (as the Dago, all hair-oil and wicked glances) with the marabou tickling his face, and the Débutante constantly surprised by what was happening to her. We had a very funny time, and the audience learned to think of me as something more than a classical dancer.

Antony Tudor also brought me down to earth in the *Lysistrata* which he made for the Ballet Club. As Myrrhina I had a frantic *pas de deux* with Walter Gore, who was playing my husband, during which I danced with our baby, which Walter tried to get away from me as he wished to dance with me alone. He would place the baby firmly on the ground, and then I would break off the *pas de deux* to rescue it, to stop it from crying.

In *Foyer de Danse* Fred came up with another lovely role for me. In this ballet he capitalized brilliantly on the smallness of the Mercury Theatre stage, with its staircase at the back, which he incorporated into the action. If we wanted to get on and off stage in this ballet we had to enter and exit by way of a window, which deposited us neatly into the street. It must have been something of a surprise for the passers-by in Notting Hill Gate to find fully costumed dancers dropping at their feet! If you did not use the window you were trapped in a dressing-room, which was little more than a tunnel of no great size or comfort, or in the wings which were not quite eighteen inches wide. *Foyer* was a ballet about ballet, about the old-fashioned French style, and I was cast as an *étoile* of the Opéra. I made my appearance wearing a hat heavy with ostrich feathers, and so generously outfitted with diamond bracelets that I did not have much time for the variation that the ballet master, Fred, was setting for me. The joke was that Fred should set me diabolically difficult steps, but that I should be so fascinated with my reflection in the mirror that I would appear to pay only the slightest attention, while actually performing them with nonchalant ease. One variation ended with me so carried away with my own skill that I finished with my back to the audience; then, realizing that I was staring at myself, I registered, "That's strange!" and turned to bow sweetly to the public. It was great fun and we—and the Mercury audiences—loved it. (There is, I am happy to say, a tiny fragment of film of *Foyer* taken at the time, which catches its atmosphere very well.)

But of all the works which Fred made at the Ballet Club, *Les Masques* seems to me the most chic and beautiful. It was also the most elegant, thanks to the wonderful designs of Sophie Fedorovich, a great friend of Mim and Fred. She created extremely witty costumes, dressing me in a white ball-gown with a train which I could gather up and carry while dancing, and giving me—ultra chic; ultra '30s—a transparent mica muff and hat, inside which could be seen the white gardenia in my hair. *Les Masques* had a 'daring' theme. It told of a diplomat and his wife (Fred and the exquisitely beautiful Pearl Argyle) who meet accidentally at a ball. Each is with a lover. I was Fred's lady friend; Walter Gore was the wife's black admirer. The piece ended with a smile: the diplomat and his wife were reunited, and Wally Gore and I paired happily off, dancing some very jazzy steps as the curtain fell.

*A studio portrait. My dress is from Patou.*

Aurora's Wedding *in 1931, during the Ballet Club's first season. From left to right: Pearl Argyle and Frederick Ashton; Andrée Howard and William Chappell; Markova and Rupert Doone; Prudence Hyman and Antony Tudor; Diana Gould and Robert Stuart.*

*Ashton's* La Péri, *with Markova and Frederick Ashton, and Pearl Argyle, Elizabeth Schooling, Andrée Howard, Maude Lloyd, Suzette Morfield, Betty Cuff.*

Carnaval *with Stanislas Idzikovski.*
*Vic-Wells Ballet, 1933.*

Les Rendezvous *with Stanislas*
*Idzikovski. Vic-Wells Ballet, 1933.*

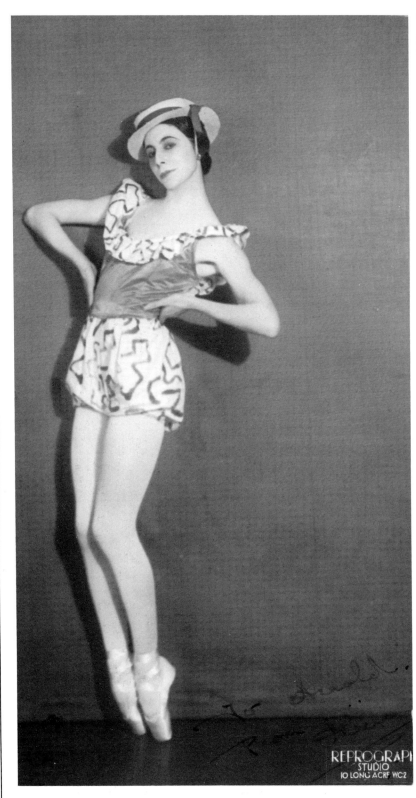

The original Polka in Façade, *for the Camargo Society, at the Cambridge Theatre, 1932.*

*Opposite: As the Débutante in* Façade *at the Ballet Club in 1933.*

REPROGRAPH
STUDIO
IO LONG ACRE WC2

At the Alhambra Theatre in 1932 in A Kiss in Spring, *dancing Frederick Ashton's Ballet of Spring, to music by Auber, and in a costume by Hedley Briggs.*

With Anton Dolin at the Coliseum in 1933, *dancing* Rondo, *a divertissement pas de deux by Ashton, to Rameau music.*

*Above:* Bar aux Folies Bergère, choreographed by *Ninette de Valois for the Ballet Club. As La Goulue, the cancan dancer, I had to appear tipsy on champagne at the end of the ballet. Ninette suggested that I study the walk of the "ladies of pleasure" in Lisle Street, and transfer this on to point for my first variation.*

*Right:* Foyer de Danse *at the Ballet Club, with dear, talented Andrée Howard.*

# The Vic-Wells Ballet 1931-35

ONE SUNDAY EVENING, LATE IN 1931, NINETTE DE VALOIS CAME back stage after a Ballet Club performance at the Mercury Theatre, and said to me that "it was about time" that I appeared with her Vic-Wells Ballet. The company was in its very first year, and Ninette wanted me to appear again in her *Cephalus and Procris* ballet which she had first staged, with me in it, during the Camargo Society season. She also intended reviving her earlier *Narcisse and Echo* for me as well. This was thought to be a very "modern" piece, with its Arthur Bliss score, its black and white decor and costumes, danced in profile (rather like *L' Après-midi d'un faune*). It made use of several levels of staging, designed to separate Narcissus from Echo. As Echo, I appeared barefoot, in slightly Wigman-esque dances, on the top of the shelf-like setting, with two nymphs half-way below me, and Narcissus obsessed with his reflection in a pool of light on stage level.

Life was becoming increasingly busy, and I was happy to find it so, despite the fragmentary nature of the work, which was shared between the Ballet Club, the Camargo Society, and now the Vic-Wells Ballet. My first performances with the company, which was to become eventually The Royal Ballet, took place in January 1932. I was soon happy to give something more than dancing, for Ninette asked me to stage *Les Sylphides*. Of course we were working with minimal forces and minimal funds, but by March 1932 Ninette could increase her twelve dancers with six more men—among them Antony Tudor— and could invite Pat Dolin to work as a more frequent guest.

In June 1932 the Ballet Club and the Vic-Wells Ballet collaborated in a two-week Camargo Society season at the Savoy Theatre. Fred Ashton revived his previous year's success, the enchanting *Lord of Burleigh*, with its delightful Mendelssohn music and George Sheringham's handsome designs, in which I danced Katie Willows. He also collaborated with the American jazz choreographer, Buddy Bradley, on *High Yellow*, for which I was coached for six weeks in jazz dancing and "the snake hips" by Buddy, who told me I reminded him of his adored Florence Mills. The key to the season, though, was the presence of Olga Spessivtseva, who danced the second act of *Swan Lake* and also *Giselle*, with Pat Dolin as her partner.

The *Giselle* was especially poignant for me: only three years earlier Diaghilev had said that he intended reviving the ballet for Spessivtseva, and that I should learn the role and dance it, too. Now I was able to study it at first hand, watching this incomparable dancer in rehearsal and sitting in the first wing each night, observing her interpretation, and learning. At the end of the second act I waited for Spessivtseva with a shawl which I placed round her shoulders, and then I accompanied her to her dressing-room. We rarely spoke. It was only on the last night of the season that she said to me, "I hope that you have watched closely. This is a ballet that will be good for you." I had adored Spessivtseva from the performances she gave with the Diaghilev Ballet, and I knew that I was seeing "the dance", pure and illuminated by the most ardent feeling. When we worked in company class with the Diaghilev Ballet, we learned that there existed certain absolute standards which we must strive to achieve if we possibly could. These are what Spessivtseva showed, never merely academically correct, but touched with soul and poetry.

Eighteen months later I was to dance *Giselle*. By this time I was the prima ballerina of the Wells company, and in the autumn of 1933 Ninette said that she was ready to stage the ballet for me. Nicholas Sergueyev, who had been in charge of productions at the Mariinsky Theatre in St. Petersburg, had fled Russia at the time of the 1917 Revolution, bringing with him large, ledger-like notebooks containing the choreographic notation and production details of the Imperial Russian Ballet's repertory. From these he was able to revive the old ballets. I rehearsed with him at Sadler's Wells Theatre in what was defined as the "board room"—a little room in which we worked each day from 10 a.m. until lunch-time. Then from 2 p.m. we rehearsed with the company in the large Wells Room that is now called The Baylis Room.

Because Sergueyev only spoke Russian and a little French, we tended to work together musically rather than by speech. When we reached certain solos in the ballet, he would offer me "alternatives", indicating at the end of the first act variation, for instance, that Spessivtseva had danced one sequence of steps, Karsavina another. He invited me to choose, and I would usually opt for Spessivtseva's text, which I had seen in performance and liked because it "moved" more. (Similarly, when we came to prepare *Swan Lake* during the autumn of the next year, Sergueyev offered me two versions of the Swan Queen's solo in the lake-side scene. One had been danced by Legnani, creator of the role, the other by Mathilde Kschessinskaya, first Russian interpreter of Odette. In the event I learned both, and combined elements from both in my performance.)

The mad scene in *Giselle* was set strictly to the music. This Sergueyev was very insistent upon, because of the timing and the fact that it was rather like an "orchestration" in that it involved not only Giselle, but also Albrecht, Bathilde, the

Duke, Hilarion and Berthe. Today, I am afraid, ballerinas tend to dance their own versions, suiting themselves entirely. When I had learned and absorbed Sergueyev's version, which was made to fit exactly, to dove-tail with the music, then, and only then could I set about becoming the mad Giselle. (In the same way all the comedy in the second act of *Coppélia* was originally very carefully set out with the music, and Sergueyev gave me the basic structure on which to work.)

Giselle did not die, as one sometimes sees today, by stabbing herself. Sergueyev explained that when Giselle feels something under her foot and looks down at the sword, she is in fact so confused that she imagines she has trodden on a snake. She picks it up without looking at it, and I was told that she weaves it along the ground in serpentine fashion because she still believes it to be a snake and brings it to her bosom as if to make the snake bite her. But it never touches her, and Giselle dies—so Sergueyev told me—from complete emotional and physical shock: in other words from a broken heart. (I checked, and I was told that medically a victim of serious shock gradually becomes cold; the circulation is affected and the heart *can* stop.) So Giselle finds that she cannot breathe. Her hands and arms become icy chill. Her chest and throat are affected. She calls for help, circling past her friends, and at last collapses on to her mother. It is then that she must make her final appeal to Albrecht. The scene is musically consistent and, though her mind is clouded, it can clear momentarily, as a cloud might lift for an instant, then darken. As Giselle feels her life ebbing away, she senses that Albrecht is near and gestures to him. She starts to mime "I ... you ...." In the middle of this she falls dead. The mime is incomplete. Albrecht can never know what she was going to say to him. Was it "forgive" or "love" or "implore"? She dies in mid-breath, and the question is unanswered. Albrecht's visit to her grave in the second act is a search for the answer to this question.

The preparations for this first English *Giselle* were careful, and we had the inestimable advantage of time in which to work on the production. It was not opulent by any means, for the Vic-Wells finances would not admit of anything save serious, basic design. This was carefully done by Barbara Allen, a young staff designer with the Vic-Wells Opera, and the production was scheduled to open the New Year: the first night was on New Year's Day 1934 at the Old Vic.

It might have been a better chosen date, as far as I was concerned: New Year's Eve revels in the house in which we lived went happily on into the small hours; I had taken to my bed in the hope of a sound early-night's rest, but I could as well have joined the party to which I had been invited, because sleep was not to be mine. Even more serious was a dank, heavy fog. All New Year's Day it thickened, and by the time I set out for the theatre London was in the grip of a throat tightening, all-obscuring pea-souper. Taxis were not to be found in the gloom that had descended by four in the afternoon, and I groped my way to the tube, feeling my route by means of railings and a few land-marks that could still be seen. By the time I reached Waterloo darkness had descended, and the worry was whether an audience would be able to get to the theatre at all. During the first ballet, *Pomona*, I was told that the seats in the theatre were filling, and I was immensely cheered to receive a first-night present from Mim Rambert—a parcel which I opened to discover the bodice worn by Karsavina in the second act of the Diaghilev *Giselle* in 1910. I took it as a happy omen for the performance. But of what transpired—from the moment I stepped out of Giselle's cottage to find Pat Dolin waiting for me as Albrecht, to the moment when the final curtain fell—I now have no memory, save for the fact that the fog crept insidiously into the theatre and, though it enhanced the mystery of the second act setting, it also caught at our lungs.

That the production was a success, and that I was more than well received in the role, is part of British ballet history, and I would be falsely naïve if I said that I did not thrill to the fact that I had proved myself worthy of this great role, or that the company had not been praised for the achievement. What was even more encouraging was that this staging seemed to indicate that the company had "arrived" and that packed houses and great enthusiasm greeted our subsequent performances. (In these I had Stanley Judson as my Albrecht, because Pat became ill with 'flu before our second performance and subsequently left to fulfil a commercial engagement, so that Robert Helpmann then became my Albrecht during the next season.)

The success of the *Giselle* staging meant more than the acquisition of an important work for the young company: it was also part of a larger plan of Ninette's to mount important nineteenth-century ballets to provide a solid classical foundation for her company and for her audience. It was my good fortune to be on hand to help in the achieving of this goal. Thus, within a month, Sergueyev had also staged *Casse-Noisette*, which made a great hit with our audience (and in it Elsa Lanchester joined as a guest from the Old Vic Theatre company for the *Danse Arabe*). From the moment *Casse* was staged, I feel that the company never looked back. Towards the end of the season Ninette also staged *The Haunted Ballroom*, in magnificent designs by Motley, with Bobby Helpmann as the Master of Treginnis, and three ghostly ladies who were named after their interpreters at the first performance: Ursula (Moreton), Beatrice (Appleyard), and Alicia.

More important still was the next great classic which Sergueyev staged: *Swan Lake* in its four acts, with all the challenges that implied. Ninette's belief in these great works also implied the fact that they could be expanded and developed when time and resources permitted. For her, though, the first and vital matter was to get them on the stage and into the consciousness of her dancers and her audience. For *Swan Lake* I gave myself a present: I went to work privately with Nicholas Legat to prepare myself for the third act. He it was who had partnered Legnani in performances of the original 1895 staging, and from her he had learned the secrets of the *fouettés*. Once again Ninette's faith was justified: here was the first staging by a young British company of one of the most important four-act ballets in the Imperial Russian repertory. It was an immense challenge, which we greeted with delight, and Bobby Helpmann as Siegfried proved an admirable partner for me.

The Haunted Ballroom, *with the Vic-Wells Ballet. Robert Helpmann as the Master of Treginnis.*

With Walter Gore as Faust and
Frederick Ashton as Mephisto in
Mephisto Waltz *at the Ballet Club in
1934.*

*Swan Lake, Act Two, with Robert Helpmann as Siegfried, and William Chappell as Benno.*

*Swan Lake, Act Three, with Robert Helpmann. Vic-Wells Ballet 1934.*

*Opposite: As Odette in* Swan Lake *with the Markova–Dolin Ballet, 1935.*

# The Markova-Dolin Ballet 1935-37

THE FORMATION OF THE MARKOVA–DOLIN BALLET CAME ABOUT through the intervention of the theatrical manager Vivian van Damm. He was a friend of my sister Doris and, soon after the Vic-Wells Ballet had staged *Swan Lake*, he came with her to a performance at the Wells. After the performance we talked about ballet, and I lamented our scheduled closure in May, for the Vic-Wells Ballet seasons ran from September to May, with a three-month summer break during which the dancers earned their livings as best they could.

Soon van Damm, with the backing of Mrs Laura Henderson, the widow of a wealthy City merchant, and van Damm's business partner, made an offer in which Mrs Henderson would underwrite an extended ballet season at the Wells after the scheduled end of the Ballet's activities, with a further transfer to the Shaftesbury Theatre for a week's season in the West End, followed by a five-week tour of the provinces playing major theatres in the Howard and Wyndham chain in our largest cities. The Vic-Wells organization would not be put to any cost for this, since Mrs Henderson would guarantee the expenses. Van Damm negotiated with Lilian Baylis, who gave us her blessing, and Van Damm Productions came into being to present this new development. Together with Mrs Henderson and Vivian van Damm, I became a director, and for the first time the Vic-Wells Ballet ventured out of its own theatres.

During our May season at the Wells we presented the first performance of Ninette's great work, *The Rake's Progress*. This was a landmark in the history of British ballet, a wonderful collaboration between the composer Gavin Gordon, Rex Whistler the designer, and Ninette, working on their Hogarthian theme. The role of the Rake was intended for Robert Helpmann, but he was already contracted, during our summer lay-off, to appear in a revue, *Stop Press,* at the Adelphi Theatre. So Walter Gore created the role, at the last moment, and had only two days notice of the fact, with the additional problem of a wisdom tooth extraction to cope with. Then Pat Dolin was invited to be *premier danseur* for the Vic-Wells season, to partner me. He signed a contract for a year, as did I, with van Damm. We moved out of London for this first provincial tour by the Vic-Wells Ballet and found a wonderfully responsive audience. But, as the tour ended, complications arose. Bobby Helpmann's revue had closed prematurely and he announced his wish to return to the company. Ninette could not afford the luxury of two principal male dancers and, with both Pat and me under contract to van Damm, there seemed a logical

*In* Les Masques *at the Ballet Club, 1933.*

Rake's Progress *with the Vic-Wells Ballet, 1935. Walter Gore as the Rake.*

move to form a company for us, following on the tremendous success we had enjoyed on the summer tour.

Thus the Markova–Dolin Ballet came into existence. We recruited more than forty dancers from the many gifted professionals in London, including leading dancers with major companies. We set about building a repertory; engaged a conductor and an orchestra; and coped with the infinity of problems which were to face us before opening night in November. Pat's temperament may have been very different from mine, but on stage we complemented each other. He was a superlative partner, with a stage presence elegant, noble, vivid. Even before the creation of this new company, the words "Markova–Dolin" had come to mean a ballet partnership to the public.

So it was that on 11 November 1935 the Markova–Dolin Ballet took the stage for the first time in Newcastle. Our repertory included the "classics"—*Swan Lake* and *Nutcracker* produced for us by Nicholas Sergueyev; *Giselle* in a production which we staged "after" Sergueyev's version; and Fokine's *Le Carnaval* and *Les Sylphides,* which we also produced. For a more personal repertory we were able to invite Keith Lester, one of our dancers, to create *David,* with a fine score by Maurice Jacobson, design by Bernard Meninsky, and a tremendous front cloth by Jacob Epstein, his unique work for the theatre. Keith also made an exquisite evocation of the *Pas de Quatre* that Jules Perrot had mounted in London in 1845 for four of the greatest ballerinas of the age. And with *Death in Adagio* Keith used Scarlatti music for what I think is the first murder-mystery ballet, in which I was a homicidal typist (in a blonde wig) who killed people with a poisoned typewriter ribbon. It made a change from *Giselle*!

During our second season, Bronislava Nijinska joined us as choreographer and ballet mistress, re-staging *Les Biches* for us, under the title *The House Party*, and *La Bien-Aimée*. She and her husband and daughter, Irina, travelled with us, and her presence was a constant inspiration. Wendy Toye, who was an eighteen-year-old dancer with us, produced her first big ballet, the touching *Aucassin and Nicolette,* with a score by Josef Holbrooke and designs by Motley. I remember that I made my entrance, as Nicolette, preceded by a ball of red wool. I had felt that I must know what Nicolette had been doing before she came on stage, and I realized that she must have been busy with her friends working on a tapestry. Hence the ball of wool, rolled on from the wings, which I pursued on stage.

These ballets, with others which we added as the year progressed, formed the repertory we danced round Britain, interspersed with seasons at the Duke of York's Theatre, our first London home. During a period of two years we gave eight performances each week. Pat and I had to dance leading roles at every performance. We could not be "off" or indisposed. Our rewards were the building of an audience, and the taking of the art we loved to a public who responded with greatest eagerness and generosity to our company. The rewards were certainly not financial. I laughed when I heard that we were sometimes supposed to be "commercial", for we each received £40 per week, from which we had to pay all our hotel accommodation, and subsistence, and provide shoes, tights, and some costumes. My life was, literally, spent between my hotel room and the stage, and my dressing-rooms were my real home. Our company was geared to work with greatest efficiency, for we sought to rationalize costs as much as possible. In the final accounting, at the end of our two years' work, it emerged that Mrs Henderson's subvention to us amounted to £1,000 per month in support of a ballet company, its orchestra, incessant touring and eight performances each week. To be more exact,

*The Markova–Dolin Ballet, with Pat on the extreme left, and next to him Bobby St John Roper, our wardrobe master. Mrs Laura Henderson is seated next to Nicholas Sergueyev.*

each performance cost Mrs Henderson approximately £50, for orchestra, dancers, stage-crew, travel, production costs.

In addition to this gruelling work, Pat and I took the chance, during a rehearsal period, to appear in a pantomime. (Fifteen years before, my career had started in pantomime, I recalled.) In *Mother Goose* at the London Hippodrome we danced an interpolated *pas de deux* to Tchaikovsky music, which Madame Nijinska helped us to arrange. The stunning principal boy was Florence Desmond—and we have remained dear friends from that day to this.

But the effect of all this intense work, and the cumulative strain of having to perform without relief, took its eventual toll. During the Coronation Summer of 1937, while our company was giving a season at our other London home, the King's Theatre Hammersmith, I developed a pain in one foot which was diagnosed as sinuvitis, symptom of the weariness brought on by the exhausting schedule of the past eighteen months. To replace me, we invited Vera Nechinova to join the company, for she and Pat had worked together before and she knew the repertory.

On the final night of the season I sat in the stage box watching the performance. At this moment Massine joined me, for he was in London with the de Basil Ballet Russe at Covent Garden. Rumours were already rife in the ballet world that Leonid was eager to break with de Basil. I soon gathered that he was to form a new Ballet Russe company, with American backing, and with Leonid himself as artistic director and Sol Hurok as impresario. I gathered, too, that Leonid was eager to invite me to join the company, and that he intended approaching Pat for the same reason. I talked matters over with Madame Nijinska, who sympathized with the amount of work I had undertaken and understood the effect of over-work on my foot. So Pat and I agreed that, after completing the scheduled tour of our company during the autumn, we would accept Massine's offer, and liquidate the company. But here fate stepped in.

We separated for our summer holidays, and I was not able to contact Pat when the time came to sign contracts with Massine. I duly signed mine, but I was to learn later that Massine had also invited Serge Lifar to appear as guest *premier danseur* for the classic productions and to stage *Giselle*, and that Pat had objected to this. He had therefore decided to join the rival Ballet Russe company, that of Colonel de Basil. It seemed that, with the ending of the Markova–Dolin Company's tour in the autumn, our partnership was ended, too.

Giselle, *1935, the first act solo. The Vic-Wells staging was redesigned by William Chappell for the summer tour. In the group of peasant girls seated on the ground at the extreme right is my sister, Berenice, while the fourth from right is Margot Fonteyn.*

Giselle *Act Two with the Markova–Dolin Ballet.*

*Opposite: Nijinska's* The Beloved One *for the Markova–Dolin Ballet, 1936, with designs by George Kirsta.*

*Nijinska re-titled* Les Biches *for the Markova–Dolin Ballet in 1936, calling it* The House Party.

*Markova–Dolin Ballet, 1935: in Keith Lester's finale for the Divertissement, my costume was designed by Mstislav Dobujinsky.*

*"La Camargo", arranged for me by Ninette de Valois in 1938 for the Royal Academy of Dancing's Production Club performance to raise money for the Academy.*

*Rehearsing at Sadler's Wells Theatre,
1934. I am wearing the woollen tights
which I always knitted for myself—
they are forerunners of today's leg-
warmers.*

# TO AMERICA
# 1938-48

# With the Ballet Russe de Monte Carlo 1938-41

*Previous page:* Giselle *Act One, with the Ballet Russe de Monte Carlo, Drury Lane, 1938.*

*Monte Carlo 1938: the beginning of* Ballet Russe de Monte Carlo *with new partners Roland Guérard, Fredric Franklin, Leonid Massine and Michel Panaieff.*

A PRESS CUTTING FOR 6 NOVEMBER 1937 TELLS OF WHAT WAS about to happen in my career.

"M. René Blum has some interesting news for the future of his ballet company. In the New Year Leonid Massine, the famous dancer, will join the company and compose several new ballets, including one based on Beethoven's Seventh Symphony. An important addition to his company is in the person of Alicia Markova, who will soon join . . ."

René Blum had started a new ballet company in Monte Carlo three years after Diaghilev's death and the disbanding of the Ballet Russe, and had initiated his company with George Balanchine as choreographer. Blum, a most delightful man, was soon joined by the very astute Colonel W. de Basil, as an associate, and by Leonid Massine, as choreographer and dancer.

Balanchine left, first to form the short-lived Ballets 1933, and then to go to America at the invitation of Lincoln Kirstein. The revived Monte Carlo Ballet Russe had an immediate success, but Blum and de Basil were not a happy partnership and eventually they separated, with Blum forming another Monte Carlo company in which he was joined by Fokine. But neither was Massine happy with de Basil, and when he left de Basil's company in 1938 there promised to be a tremendous realignment of forces in the Russian Ballet, in which I was now

involved. Massine had urged me as early as 1932 to leave Britain and work with the Monte Carlo company, which he thought was my "home". I then felt that my "home" was with the young British ballet, at the Mercury Theatre, at the Vic-Wells, and with the Camargo Society, where I could be of unique service. Now after five years, and with the added achievements of our Markova–Dolin Ballet, Leonid again invited me to join him in the new enterprise being formed round the existing Blum company. Massine again said I should feel "at home", and indeed I did, for Monte Carlo was itself like home, and I found many dear friends—Choura Danilova, of course, and Leonid, and Freddie Franklin, our protégé from the Markova–Dolin company, as well as new colleagues and partners: Igor Youskevich for *Seventh Symphony*; Roland Guérard for *Bluebird* and *Le Carnaval*; Michel Panaieff for *Swan Lake, Coppélia, Les Elfes* and *L'Epreuve d'Amour*.

This was an extraordinary time for the Ballets Russes companies, with dancers shuttling between de Basil and Blum/Massine, and even Fokine going back briefly to de Basil because Massine was in artistic control of the new Ballet Russe de Monte Carlo (a name automatically inherited, and greatly valued, by our impresario, Sol Hurok). Massine brought ballets from his de Basil period, as well as from the Diaghilev years. We had Fokine works. Toumanova joined from de Basil; Slavenska from Paris; Theilade from Hollywood; while Fokine had initially brought Krassovska and Panaieff to Monte Carlo. If people today are confused by the changes of personnel and titles (I signed contracts for the Massine company with both "World Art" and "Universal Art" companies), I am not surprised for we—in the middle of it all—were confused, too, never quite sure who was where, with whom, for what, for how long.

In addition to the new roles which were to come to me, Massine wished me to dance Giselle, and he had invited Serge Lifar as guest artist from the Paris Opéra (whose ballet company Lifar directed) to produce the ballet and to dance Albrecht. Lifar was used to his own version of the Romantic masterpiece, and I was soon to realize that his views, which stressed the importance of Albrecht, and mine, which were the result of my work with Nicholas Sergueyev and with Spessivtseva, were very different. I knew that my version was correctly within the traditions of the Imperial Russian Ballet—which had saved *Giselle* itself from oblivion—but Serge was eager to cut certain beautiful sequences in order to concentrate upon Albrecht's reactions to the drama, even in the mad scene. I also

Giselle *Act One, with Igor Youskevich
as Albrecht in the Ballet Russe de
Monte Carlo staging at Drury Lane,
1938. I am wearing the "Bakst"
costume which came to the rescue in the
Benois setting.*

*In the summer of 1984 Serge Lifar sold part of his collection at Sotheby's, and we were photographed in front of his portrait in* Les Matelots *by Pedro Pruna.*

Giselle *Act One, with the Ballet Russe de Monte Carlo, Drury Lane, 1938, with Serge Lifar.*

Giselle, *Act Two, with the Ballet
Russe de Monte Carlo, at the Theatre
Royal, Drury Lane, London, 1938,
with Alexandra Danilova as Myrtha.*

*With my dear Choura at her country
home in 1940, and in 1976 at the
Pavlova Museum, Ivy House, London,
seated in front of Pavlova's theatrical
dressing-table which was bequeathed to
me and which I have loaned to the
museum.*

knew that I could not return to London (where the Ballet Russe de Monte Carlo was to have its first big season) in a production so different in its approach from the old ballet's qualities. We started rehearsals rather warily. We were fortunate that Alexandre Benois (who had loved *Giselle* since his childhood in St Petersburg fifty years before) was responsible for the designs. I also had the joy of knowing that Choura Danilova had asked to dance Queen of the Wilis at my performances; with her presence I knew that we were maintaining the best traditions of the ballet.

The first night in London, at Drury Lane, was dramatic.

*Outside the Café de Paris, Monte Carlo, 1938.*

Although I was scheduled and announced for the first performance, the wardrobe had—curiously—made costumes only for Toumanova, who was to dance Giselle later in the week. I was thus presented with costumes which fitted only where they touched. I took a firm stand, saying to Massine that he must announce to the public that I was ready to dance, warmed up—indeed, spiritually I was very warmed up—but my costumes were not available. As the minutes passed, I suddenly remembered that I had my Bakst costumes from the Markova–Dolin company production, which could be quickly brought to the theatre. Despite Lifar's protestations that he could not have his production "ruined" by my wearing anything but the Benois designs, Sol Hurok announced that of course I should dance in my own costumes. I was now distraught, and weeping, but, helped by dear Choura and by the unexpected appearance of Baron (then a young photographer) who persuaded me to have a few sips of brandy to calm me, I was determined to dance. The audience may have been restive because of the unexpected delay before the ballet, but they greeted me with such warmth on my entrance that I knew that I would not disappoint them.

At the end of the evening the curtain calls were heartening. The audience expected me to take a solo call. But Serge did not seem to understand this, and I can do no better than quote from the *News Chronicle* account which appeared the next morning.

> Serge Lifar, specially imported from Paris, seemed more intent upon advertising himself than Markova. Her dancing last night was so diamond bright, and her acting so restrained, that this emphasised what London audiences already know: that there is no finer classical dancer in the world. She did this against the heavy handicap of a partner whose intensive efforts at feats of elevation and display made anything but a satisfactory background. The performances ended with a campaign waged relentlessly by the gallery to separate Markova from her partner and give her her belated due. After 10 ferocious minutes, they succeeded. It was nice to be on their side.

I imagine that Serge, accustomed to the tremendous receptions which were his due at the Paris Opéra, could not appreciate that, for the London public, I was coming home. Alas, he had to be physically restrained by two stage hands in order that the theatre might calm down, while I received the public's thanks, and showed mine.

Christian Bérard was a stage designer and artist of greatness. His work was simple, beautiful. While we were dancing in Monte Carlo during the first season of the new Ballet Russe de Monte Carlo in 1938, Bérard came to prepare the designs for Massine's *Seventh Symphony*. The plan for the ballet was very modern and very clear, as were the decor and costumes that Bérard gave us. I was the Spirit of the Air and Sky, and Bérard designed a ravishing costume of all-over white silk tights with, over them, a sensational chiffon skirt which was cut "on the cross" with invisible white horse-hair woven in to it so that the fabric moved like clouds. The silk chiffon of the skirt was a clear sky-blue with faintest pink clouds appliquéd on to it. It fastened at the waist with a blue and pink band, while a cloud was also appliquéd on my breast, covering one shoulder. The costume was a work of art, easy to dance in, and of exquisite beauty—such creations have largely disappeared from ballet today.

On the opening night, I was at the Casino Theatre in my dressing-room—which was little more than a cupboard—wearing tights, shoes, made-up, ready to go on stage, and aware that the previous ballet was just ending. But without my skirt. Barbara Karinska, the couturière, was notoriously late in delivering costumes (which were always perfectly made) and, as the ten-minute bell rang to warn us of curtain rise on *Seventh Symphony*, I started to get very nervous indeed.

Karinska and her helper finally appeared with the skirt—a perfect and lovely creation. But where was the costume top? And the little white wings to go in my hair? No one seemed to know about these. I pointed out that I was due on stage at the very beginning of the ballet. Suddenly Bérard entered with Boris Kochno, having heard no doubt that I was more than a little *agitata*. What was to be done? Bérard turned to Karinska and said, "Give me chiffon." Karinska's assistant had brought none, and at this moment Bérard saw on a hanger on the wall my evening dress for the party which inevitably followed a first night. There with it was a large pale-blue chiffon handkerchief—very *à la mode* in the late '30s. "Quick! Needle! Thread! Voilà!" And grabbing my handkerchief, Bérard draped and stitched it on me with amazing speed and then demanded some white paper. He snipped with my scissors, and there were two wings for my hair. He drew on them with my black eye-brow pencil, pinned them in my hair, and I took the stage as the Sky in the most instant of Bérard creations.

But this was not the only drama. I had a quick change into the third movement. I was cut out of my sky-blue top and re-

# Christian Bérard

*With Igor Youskevich in the third movement of Massine's* Seventh Symphony *for the Ballet Russe de Monte Carlo in 1938, as the God and Goddess of Air.*

dressed, when it was discovered that my head-dress of rainbow flowers had not been delivered. By greatest good fortune I had, that morning, bought in Monte Carlo a modern tiara made of opalescent paillettes. This was pressed into service for the first night and did very well, but the next day Bérard and I went shopping and bought artificial flowers at a boutique just by the old Sporting Club, and I went home and made my own head-dress—to Bérard's delighted approval.

My American debut at the Metropolitan Opera House, New York, brought me a new audience who responded with warmth to the work of the Ballet Russe de Monte Carlo and to my roles with the company. The coast-to-coast tours were interspersed with big seasons in New York, an exhausting schedule, but a rewarding one. The younger members of the company, though, were so poorly paid—no one ever got rich in the ballet in those days!—that they had to play what was known as the "Army Game" in many towns on tour. One person would book into an hotel, and six others would creep up to the room, bribe the maid to bring extra towels and other necessities, and camp there for the night. Only by this means could they actually afford to stay in an hotel at all.

For the late spring of 1939 we returned to Europe, and the Monte Carlo season which was essential if the company were to retain its Monte Carlo title. After the summer break there was to be the Covent garden season, due to start on 4 September. Danilova and I had arrived early, for Choura loved London and I was already there with my mother and sisters, since Pat Dolin had organized a few concert performances for us. But as August progressed and the international situation grew more tense, I became very worried. I was contracted to the Ballet Russe, but I was British, and on the morning of 3 September, after Mr Chamberlain's speech, I knew that I should stay in England. Danilova and I next decided that we should try and do some form of war-work. We first thought that we might become midwives and thus release nurses for wartime service. We were told that this would never do, and eventually we found work serving coffee and washing-up for the men in a government establishment in St John's Wood—but this was also then declared "unsuitable" for ballerinas.

My solicitors also told me that I must honour my contract with the Ballet Russe, and Sol Hurok spoke plainly, declaring that he would injunct me from appearing anywhere, as I was already announced for the Metropolitan Opera House season in New York, and America was not at war. He had arranged passage for Danilova and me on the S.S. *Manhattan,* which was the last American boat to leave for New York, so that we might reach New York in time for the season.

So I returned to the United States in a boat, among whose other passengers were Artur Rubinstein and his family, Paul Robeson and his family, and a group of dancers on their way to join either de Basil in Australia or the newly-formed Ballet Theatre in America—they included Antony Tudor, Hugh

Laing, Andrée Howard, Pat Dolin, Irina Baronova and her husband, Gerry Sevastianov, and Paul Petroff. The boat was crammed, and Irina Baronova and I shared a cabin with four generations of Irishwomen: great-grandmother, grandmother, mother and baby. It was rather like the Marx Brothers' cabin in *A Night at the Opera*.

I arrived in America literally penniless. Dancers, as I have said, and even leading ballerinas of a great company, were miserably paid, and Hurok's business manager, David Libidins, was at the New York docks to greet me with an advance of twenty dollars (then the equivalent of £4) to tide me over. I found it ironic that a singer or an actress with a public comparable to mine could earn thousands of dollars a week. But for all of us in the ballet the rewards were artistic rather than financial. When, as occasionally happened, people reproached me for "leaving England", I had to smile. It was my bank which obliged me to leave my country, where I could not work, in order to find a livelihood where I might use the gifts I had been given. Not for us the luxury of nights off, or performances alternating with opera nights, but a regular eight or nine performances a week, travelling through North and South America in the process. This was far too taxing a routine for dancers, and eventually our union, A.G.M.A., instituted better terms and conditions of work for the ballet. (There is, somewhere, a snapshot of me taken by André Eglevsky while on tour with Ballet Theatre. I am asleep in the gutter, with my head on my hat box, and with Jerome Robbins' and John Kriza's overcoats over my legs, waiting for a bus to take us to our next performance.)

When we arrived in New York in that autumn of 1939 Massine was profoundly relieved that Hurok had arranged for Choura and me to travel, for we had to set about rehearsing an "American" Ballet Russe de Monte Carlo, in case members of the original company, who had been scattered across Europe on holiday during August, could not get away from France where they were stranded at the outbreak of war. Of the "real" company there were only Danilova, Massine and myself; we started to work with a completely fresh company, whose members included André Eglevsky. Gradually some artists started to filter through from Europe, and we thus contrived a company that would be able to sustain the Met. season and the ensuing tour. Just in time, on the very morning that our Met. season was to open, a boat arrived from France with a cargo of Ballet Russe dancers, and that night the audience did not know which "half" of the company was to dance.

In the event the American section only danced the first ballet.

Europe was now, of course, closed to the Ballet. Hurok had to find other dates for us. So it was arranged in 1940 that after our traditional New York season we would go by boat to Rio, and undertake a lengthy tour of South America. The tour was carefully arranged to take maximum advantage from every stop. From Rio we would go to Sao Paulo, and then to smaller places such as Santos, and thence to Buenos Aires. At Santos, for example, we gave a matinee and evening performance, then took the boat to Buenos Aires. So, for me, Santos is just a memory of the smell of coffee and orchids, and the snake farm. From Buenos Aires, in turn, we made trips to smaller cities such as Rosario, then went across to Montevideo, travelling by night ferry, sleeping in berths, and arriving to give matinee and evening performances before returning to Buenos Aires in time for morning class. It was exhausting—not helped by fearful changes in temperature, from a sweltering 120 degrees with humidity, to Novemberish chills and fogs so that the male dancers would drink a glass of mulled wine to warm themselves before class. Nor was it helped by other dramas.

We were vaccinated in New York before the journey and, to avoid unsightly marks on our arms if the serum "took", the vaccination was given in our legs. I protested, but in vain. We embarked for Rio—a three week trip—and I felt well enough, sharing a "first class" cabin (the size of an average broom-cupboard) with Choura. As we went south and the weather grew hotter, I developed a fever and my leg swelled to double its size. The doctor diagnosed a delayed reaction from the vaccination, and I lay on deck with what felt like a wooden limb while other Hurok artists going on this South American venture—Artur Rubinstein and his family, Jan Kiepura and his wife Marta Eggert—commiserated with me.

In Rio the temperature was 100 degrees in the shade and streamingly humid. We were advised to drink only bottled water and to take salt tablets—and were also warned of the dangers of the white slave traffic, and of the fact that we might contract syphilis from the glasses in cafés. But there were worse problems than these. I was sufficiently recovered to be able to dance *Swan Lake* on the opening night, though other members of the company were laid low with dysentery, the results of the vaccination, and illness brought on by the variable hygiene of Rio. But Massine and Hurok, and our director Serge Denham (he had taken over from René Blum, who remained in France and was soon to die in Auschwitz) knew that con-tracts with various theatres depended upon the appearance of listed principals of the company and even upon a certain complement of dancers in any given ballet. Failure to fulfil these conditions meant that the contract could be void and payment withheld. Thus, no matter how ill they might feel, dancers had to get on stage if they possibly could.

On the second night of the season, I was dancing Giselle with Igor Youskevich as Albrecht and Choura as Myrtha, and the evening was to end with the Polovtsian Dances from *Prince Igor* led by Freddie Franklin. Just before curtain-time, Hurok appeared looking very worried. The efforts of opening night had made more members of the company ill, and there were not enough dancers to make up the proper complement for *Prince Igor*. We rallied round and agreed—on condition that our anonymity was respected, and also on condition that Massine joined the ranks of the warriors—to make up the required numbers. Choura and I knew the corps dances from our time with Diaghilev, and we were able to talk Mia Slavenska and others through the choreography. The men were rather more individualistic and, as there was no time for rehearsal, when Igor turned one way, Massine was probably turning the other. Freddie Franklin was most surprised at his supporting cast—probably the grandest the Polovtsian Dances have ever had, if not the most co-ordinated.

Meeting Artur Rubinstein and his family again was a great joy, and I was later to have the equal joy of dancing to his accompaniment during the time that Pat Dolin and I were in Hollywood during the war. Everyone used to give their services to Bette Davis' Hollywood Canteen for G.I.s, and they did the same in New York at the Stage Door Canteen. (It was there that I jitterbugged with the U.S. Coastguards' champion, "Killer Joe", a superlative natural dancer who looked rather like Massine, and who had earned his name from the fact that in jitterbug competitions he was said to "kill" his opponent on the dance floor with his exceptional stamina. I managed to keep up with him.) One Sunday afternoon in Hollywood, the Canteen decided to put on a classical programme. Rubinstein and Heifetz, Lauritz Melchior and Helen Traubel, Pat and I, were asked to perform, with Rubinstein providing all our accompaniments, as well as playing solos. Pat and I danced the Grande Valse *pas de deux* from *Les Sylphides*. We were appearing in a vast hangar-like building and, as Rubinstein began to play and Pat held me high in the lift which begins the choreography, I have a vivid memory of looking down on to a sea of white-bandaged stretcher cases who had been brought in and laid out in rows so that they might enjoy the programme.

*With Leonid Massine in his* Vienna
1814: *Turandot and the Unknown
Prince. Ballet Russe de Monte Carlo,
1940.*

Rouge et Noir *with the Ballet Russe
de Monte Carlo, 1939. Set to
Shostakovich's first symphony, this
ballet was choreographed by Massine
and designed by Matisse. I am
surrounded by André Eglevsky, Igor
Youskevich and Frederic Franklin.
Igor and I are Man and Woman,
threatened by forces of Evil.*

Despite the glamour and excitement of our New York seasons, much of the bread-and-butter for the Ballet Russe de Monte Carlo came from the company's existence on coast-to-coast tours across the United States and Canada. Because ballet was, in the late 1930s, still an uncertain commercial proposition outside the larger cities, we often played one-night stands, or short engagements, and travelling was an integral and often excruciating part of our life. The problems and practicalities of these tours sometimes meant that we did not have a single free day for weeks. We would arrive in a town to open on Friday night, then give matinee and evening performances on Saturday and Sunday, and then take the train that night to journey on to the next city and perform there on Monday night. For this hard labour the corps de ballet received thirty dollars (the equivalent then of £6) per week. The company only accepted these gruelling conditions because of a faith in our art. We all believed that we were doing something to help ballet establish itself across America: it was a matter of pride for us to dance our very best, no matter what the conditions or the nature of the theatre.

During the war years we were sometimes expected to travel by bus, and it was then our Union had to step in and decide how long a dancer might be expected to sit with legs and body cramped in a bus before getting out to dance with muscles in poor condition and injury the possible (and probably the inevitable) result. Whatever the conditions, though, we were expected to live up to the image of the "glamorous" Russian Ballet, to look immaculate and to dance immaculately.

Life was exceptionally awkward when we did not sleep in an hotel for a couple of weeks or more, because of the routine of one-night stands. We would arrive in a town, travelling in special coaches which were joined on to the regular rail service; leave the train to go to the theatre, set up the show, perform; and, while the stage hands were packing our scenery and lighting, the dancers would find a drug-store in which to eat; then we en-trained for the next city. Through all this we had to keep ourselves in fit condition to dance such demanding ballets as *Giselle, Coppélia, Swan Lake* and the Fokine and Massine repertory. There were myriad difficulties, not least laundry. As we walked through "our" railway carriage, we would see in the rest-room two dozen pairs of pink silk stage tights hanging up to dry like a forest of legs swaying as the train raced through the night. (There were no easy-care fabrics, then; no nylon.)

One learned hard but very important lessons about the

# On Tour

obligation to one's public, about surviving, about oneself as an artist. Supremely, one had to remember, as one rattled along to some township, that there was an audience who had waited perhaps for more than a year to see the ballet. They might have travelled many miles to see me; I had to give them the best of myself for they deserved nothing less.

There were occasions when we could not get back to our train until two in the morning, after scenery and lights had been manhandled back from the theatre to the carriages, and the dancers had to while away the hours in the local drug-store, which our management would persuade the owner to keep open late so that we might eat—usually ham and eggs (which was the title we gave to our traditional triple bill on these tours) and buckets of coffee.

Our orchestra had its own coach; the stage crew and scenery had two coaches; there was a costume coach for the wardrobe;

*In* Giselle *Act Two, with Dolin, in the Ballet Russe de Monte Carlo production, 1940.*

and we dancers had another couple of coaches. These five or six carriages were hitched on to trains in the railway schedules. And thus we gypsied our way across America.

*Coppélia* and *The Nutcracker* were favourite ballets on these journeys and, though it may have become tedious for the corps de ballet to perform the same works every night, the principals kept fresh by alternating performances. *Coppélia* was, of course, Choura Danilova's: her champagne quality was adorable in it. Mia Slavenska was the second cast and Massine asked me to be the other Swanilda, with Igor Youskevich as my usual Franz. *Nutcracker* was "my" ballet, with the other ballerinas also alternating the lead, though I seemed often to have to give long unbroken series of performances. Of course there were odd incidents. In Dallas, Texas, Igor and I had gone to the cinema since Choura and Freddie Franklin were dancing *Coppélia* that evening. We were "tourists"—which was what the company called dancers who had a night off. But half-way through the film we were called urgently from the cinema by the management. Both Choura and Freddie had fallen victim to the local drinking water and, though they had managed to get through the first two acts of *Coppélia*, they could not continue, and Igor and I (who had mercifully done our warm-up before going out for the evening) completed the ballet.

One of the worst features of these tours was the absence of baths. Choura and I always checked the schedule of the tour and, if we arrived early in the afternoon in a town, we took a suite in the local hotel for the day—hotels offered "day rates". We went to our rooms and promptly tipped the maid five dollars (which was a fortune in those days) and asked for piles of towels. We each had a long, blissful bath and thereafter, at fifteen minute intervals, the boys and girls of the company would come up from the hotel lobby, where they had stationed themselves, to take the opportunity to soak some of the aches from their bodies. Thus we kept our spirits up, and were also able to get away from drug-store food. Often during the last ballet of the evening, when the audience might suppose us deeply engrossed in our roles, there would be a barrage of whispers. "Where do we eat?" "Marc Platt says that, when he was here last time, there was a good restaurant on Main Street." "O.K. You get there first. We'll join you as soon as possible." And we would nip through the closing scene of *Coppélia* or *Nutcracker*.

Leonid Massine kept rather apart from this touring life. He used in the early days to travel with a huge car, a caravan attached behind as living quarters. He had a chauffeur-cum-chef, for food was essential to Leonid, and he had developed a way of touring through America from his earlier visits there with the de Basil Ballet. His caravan was my dressing-room on more than one occasion, memorably on a fierce winter night in Eugene, Oregon, with no theatre other than the High School auditorium, and no hotel. The auditorium had but one dressing-area, not very near the stage. As we started the performance snow, which had already been falling, turned into a blizzard. Leonid's caravan, parked against the back door of the hall, served as wings for those of us waiting to go on stage, and I stood in it preparatory to making my entrance as Odette in *Swan Lake*, Act Two, which was the opening ballet, while Leonid, dressed and made-up as the Peruvian in his own *Gaieté Parisienne,* started on the meal he always ate before a performance. (Unlike any other dancer I have known, Massine needed to stoke up his energies immediately before appearing.) I descended to the shores of the enchanted lake pursued by the delicious smells of Leonid's dinner and found the corps de ballet so crowded on the stage that they had to back into the wings to give Mischa Panaieff and me room for the great *adagio*. But the Ballet Russe de Monte Carlo was contracted to appear, and appear we did—blizzards, and every other inconvenience, notwithstanding.

In some small towns the theatre was also a cinema. Sometimes, when we arrived early in a town with nothing to see except the drug-store and the shops on Main Street, the dancers would make for the cinema to while away a couple of hours before warming up and performance. On one occasion, Mischa Paneyev and I were scheduled once again to open the ham-and-eggs programme with *Swan Lake* in a cinema-theatre. A couple of hours before curtain up, we went on stage to prepare, only to find the cinema owner telling our manager, David Libidins (who was part Russian, part Turk, and wholly paternal), that the ballet could not be set as there was still an audience in the house watching the film. Mischa and I returned to our dressing-rooms, and Libidins told the cinema owner that at 7 p.m. the film *must* end so that the Ballet might get ready for its 8 o'clock curtain. At 7 p.m. the film was still showing. Libidins demanded that the house-lights be put up, and he went in front of the screen and addressed the audience with his usual opening word "*Publicum!* Show over, otherwise no ballet tonight." At this moment the audience for the film was revealed—it was made up of members of the ballet. Libidins was furious and, for weeks after, dancers were forbidden to go to the cinema before performance.

With André Eglevsky in the first staging of The Nutcracker—by the Ballet Russe de Monte Carlo in 1940—in America. I had also danced the very first Nutcracker in England. This delightful ballet went on to conquer America, and has become indestructible.

As Swanilda in Coppélia with the Ballet Russe de Monte Carlo, in 1939.

# At Jacob's Pillow 1941

IN 1941 THE IMPRESARIO SOL HUROK, WHO HAD A CONTROLLING hand on the touring destinies of ballet companies in America, decided to relinquish his interest in the Ballet Russe de Monte Carlo and promote Ballet Theatre, which had been founded by Lucia Chase just two years before. Sol was aware that my contract with the Ballet Russe was ending, and he sent Pat Dolin to see me, to urge me not to re-join the Monte Carlo troupe—with whom I could have named my own price—but to consider signing with Ballet Theatre. Both Mikhail Fokine and Leonid Massine were joining it; Antony Tudor was already with the company; many new roles would be created for me; and I would be reunited with Pat as my partner for the classics. My Ballet Russe contract ended in May, and Hurok planned to take Ballet Theatre, with me, under his wing at the beginning of the new season, in September 1941, preparing for appearances at the Metropolitan Opera House in New York, and for coast to coast tours.

But how to keep Ballet Theatre together during the summer months? There came the idea of using Jacob's Pillow, Ted Shawn's property in Massachussetts, where the father of American Dance had lived and worked with his group of Men Dancers since the 1930s. The Men Dancers had built log cabins and a barn surrounding the main house where Ted lived, and this had been the centre for his creativity. Now it seemed that Ted was in some financial difficulties, and he and Pat met and talked. Since it was impossible for us to return to Europe, the idea came of a Summer School, with the opportunity to invite Ballet Theatre to be "in residence" and work there. My friend Reginald Wright leased Jacob's Pillow for me from Ted, who joined us in this very first Summer School, which Pat directed, while Ballet Theatre was also able to live, work and rehearse there. My task, besides rehearsing, was to take charge of feeding the horde of dancers and students, and my weekly fee for this was ten dollars. Ballet Theatre's dancers went on unemployment benefit, which amounted to ten dollars a week, and they contributed a dollar a day for board and lodging, retaining three dollars as spending money. Lucia Chase joined us, as did Bronislava Nijinska and her daughter, Antony Tudor and Hugh Laing, Irina Baronova and her husband, Gerry Sevastianov, who was company manager for Ballet Theatre. They were found homes locally, billetted on families whom Ted Shawn recommended.

New ballets were put into rehearsal, before Hurok sent the company off to Mexico City for a trial run to prepare us for the New York season. At Jacob's Pillow the organizing of

*As the Queen of Hearts in Balanchine's* Poker Game *for the Ballet Russe de Monte Carlo in 1940, costume by Irene Sharaff. This strange pose was Balanchine's idea at the photographic sitting.*

*At Jacob's Pillow, 1941.*

With Pat, sweeping the main studio. Studying our brochure for the Summer School. I was already wearing pants for working and travel, which later became very fashionable. Behind us is Ted Shawn's house.

We celebrated Freddie Franklin's birthday at Jacob's Pillow in 1941 with a Square Dance. Pat and I, Sammy Spring (the famous "caller"), Nora Kaye, and, kneeling, Nana Gollner and Annabel Lyon.

*"The Sylphide and the Scotsman" pas de deux, which we choreographed.*

*As the Sylphide. This photograph was taken at seven o'clock in the morning to catch the right effect of light.*

"the feeding of the five thousand"—as it seemed to me—nearly produced nervous collapse, but we had a splendid master cook, Capp, who came with breakfast to my room each morning at 8 o'clock, when we planned the day's menus, while the mothers of the six young girl students who were also part of our complement were invaluable in helping to look after the girls, and even ran the box office for the afternoon performances we gave. These, despite the stringencies of petrol rationing, brought in a flood of visitors, from as far away as New York, and photographers—of the eminence of Horst, Hoyningen-Huene—flocked at the week-ends to work with us and join in the Sunday "open house" when Capp provided a feast of roast beef, with all the proper trimmings, for dancers, students, journalists and well-wishers who came to see this extraordinary new community. The enterprise was, I think, successful both in its first object of keeping Ballet Theatre's dancers together, and in creating a "family" atmosphere, which was important as we worked, and worked again, for the forthcoming season.

# Working with Fokine 1941-42

I FIRST WORKED WITH MIKHAIL FOKINE WHEN I JOINED BALLET Theatre—this was one of the inducements which led me to leave the Ballet Russe de Monte Carlo. Ballet Theatre had a new production of *Les Sylphides,* a brand new ballet, *Bluebeard,* and as it turned out, *The Dying Swan* which Fokine asked me to dance. Later, as we worked with the Maestro in Mexico, he coached me in *Petrushka* and *Le Spectre de la rose* which I had already danced with many partners in the Ballet Russe.

Fokine had never returned to the Diaghilev Ballet after his split with Diaghilev in 1914, but Serge Grigoriev had always talked about him, telling us, when roles were passed on, that Fokine wanted *this* or *that*. When I first joined the Ballet Russe de Monte Carlo I had danced several more recent Fokine works, which were taught by the *régisseur* Jean Jazvinsky, including *Les Elfes* and *L'Epreuve d'Amour,* in which I danced Nemchinova's role. *L'Epreuve* was a ballet full of delicate humour, with beautiful Chinoiserie designs by André Derain, set to an exquisite Mozart score. It was a work which we danced a great deal on the first Ballet Russe tour—and never danced again! We returned to Europe from America in the spring of 1939 on the S.S. *Rex,* ready for the Monte Carlo season. As we disembarked at Cannes, the captain grew impatient while the scenery was being unloaded. Sets and costumes were dumped into the harbour where, alas, they remain, and the ballet was never again performed.

Now in New York in 1941 I came in personal contact with the master choreographer for the first time. To me he was a very great man, part of the grand lineage of Russian ballet masters. Somehow, from his choreography, I was expecting a very generous-natured person but, though he was always kind to me, I noticed that he could be sarcastic to certain dancers. One might not receive praise or much encouragement, but I was mature enough to understand that, whatever bitterness he felt, one had to ignore this and endeavour to learn all that one could from this genius. When he discovered that nothing seemed to ruffle me, we contrived to get along in a quiet and undemonstrative way.

At our first private rehearsal for *Les Sylphides* in New York, he sat on a chair in the middle of the studio and asked me, "Please dance. Show me what you have." I enquired which variation he would like to see, and told him that at different times in my career I had danced all three variations: the first Waltz, the Mazurka, and the Prelude; but that I had been most usually cast in the Mazurka. I danced each solo for him, then the *pas de deux* with George Skibine as my partner. Fokine sat very sternly, and watched without giving any corrections. Then he said, "So this is *Les Sylphides?*".

I answered that it was what I had watched and learned with Diaghilev, but he went on, "It is not really *Sylphides.*" I immediately asked, "Then please, Maestro, show me what *is.*" From the next rehearsal he did exactly that, instructing me in every nuance of timing, phrasing, musical understanding. I had danced the ballet a great deal, staged it for the Vic-Wells Ballet, danced it with Diaghilev under Grigoriev's instruction. I had seen many great dancers in it, including Karsavina. But I had never really enjoyed dancing *Les Sylphides* as I felt I should, even though Bronislava Nijinska had been wonderfully helpful in passing on to me the Mazurka which she had danced for Fokine with the Diaghilev company.

Now Fokine said that I should learn all three variations, and that he would then decide which one I should dance with Ballet Theatre. Eventually he chose the Prelude. It was choreography which, he explained to me, must be thought about very differently from the straight lines of, say, Petipa. Fokine wanted curves. He called *Les Sylphides* "a romantic reverie", and this was the key to the piece. Exits were not exits, for you had to leave the stage as if you were reaching for the moon. "Reach, reach!" he would shout. "The moon is up *there!* You are reaching to try and touch the moon!" He taught me that you have to pass completely beyond technique—even throw it away. People may think that *Les Sylphides* is easy, but it is one of the most difficult of ballets because what is needed is tremendous technical strength which must then be concealed and become second nature. There are no preparations for the steps; they just happen. Everything has to be sustained, floating. No effort must be seen, ever. Each step has its meaning. There is no beginning or end to movements—they melt away like sound on the air. Fokine asked this of hundreds of dancers, but said that they either could not, or would not, achieve the effects he wanted. Of the entrances he said, "You should suddenly be there—the audience should not see you come on stage." The poet seeks to restrain you from flying away, which is why he holds you. Sylphides have the ability to float away, and they are only seen in this moonlit glade because they wish to be there.

Very strict and specific about the timing of each moment in the ballet, Fokine wanted his dancers to listen to the music and to give the effect that the whole scene was spontaneous. He never wished one to be aware of the audience. A small incident was very illuminating. As I rehearsed the reprise of the *pas de*

*Fokine's* Bluebeard *for Ballet Theatre in 1941: Princess Hermilia, with George Skibine as Prince Sapphire, at the end of the ballet. The costumes were by Marcel Vertès.*

*deux*, where I had always been led to believe (and observed with other ballerinas) that a gesture was made to the floor, Fokine shouted, "What are you looking for? What have you lost?" I replied that this was how I had been taught to perform the moment. "Not so," he said. "You look at each other, and then look away to the corps de ballet." At last I learned what the ballet was about, and for the first time felt comfortable, with the *real* choreography.

In New York, Ballet Theatre started working with Fokine on *Bluebeard*. It was a wild comedy in which I was cast as a Princess, who is lost as a child and brought up by peasants, but who is claimed finally as her rightful self. There was a stellar cast led by Pat Dolin as Bluebeard, with Irina Baronova, Lucia Chase, Rosella Hightower, Annabelle Lyon, Jerome Robbins and Antony Tudor. The designs were by Marcel Vertès and the head-dresses were executed by John Fredericks. (I was dressed as a young Italian girl, with two black braids made of wool.) Fokine knew that I had a large classic repertory and he devised comedy from playing me against my usual image, as in the can-can on point in which I travelled across the stage holding up my long white skirt, performing thirty-two high *relevés*. George Skibine was my partner as a young Prince disguised as a shepherd, and we were given a beautiful *pas de deux*. At the end of the first scene there was a Tarantella which took the cast off stage, leaving George and me behind, and we had to finish by falling flat on our backs, legs kicking in the air. I was soon achingly bruised, because we performed the ballet a great deal and every night we had to end with this jolting fall. What the audience did not see was the padding I devised to try and protect myself from becoming permanently black and blue.

Fokine also paid me a beautiful compliment by asking me to dance *The Dying Swan,* which he had made for Anna Pavlova more than thirty years before. He revised the dance specially for me, coaching me carefully and insisting that there were no "mechanics" in the dance. It was as if the swan were trying to fly but could not, and in the control of the effects that he wanted there lay all the difficulties of this short, intense drama which one had to conceal from the audience, so that they saw simply the last heart-breaking moments of the swan.

*This is how Acapulco looked in 1942, when it was a fishing village. Behind me in the surf is Jerome Robbins. Right: In Guadelajara, on the Ballet Theatre Mexican tour in 1942. With Pat Dolin.*

THE CHOICE OF MARC CHAGALL AS DESIGNER FOR MASSINE'S *Aleko* (which was inspired by Pushkin's poem *Gypsies*) was due to Henry Clifford, curator of the Philadelphia Museum. A man of great culture and charm, he was, at the time I joined Ballet Theatre, artistic advisor to the company. I had met him previously at his beautiful villa in Florence, and now, in Mexico City, with so much artistic creativity and so many distinguished designers at work, I was reminded of the days of the Diaghilev Ballet, with Clifford like one of those artistic counsellors who surrounded Diaghilev.

Chagall designed a white costume for me as Zemphira, the gypsy girl, in the first scene, and on this he painted the decoration himself. On the bodice, just below my heart, he painted a heart and beneath it drew the Tree of Life. Chagall adored fantasy, and whenever he sent me messages he signed them with a heart and his name inside it—saying he gave me his heart each time, which was a typically happy idea. He designed armlets and jewels for Zemphira made from gold coins, and these he let me make for myself, just as he did when next we worked on *The Firebird*—the new production which Adolf Bolm mounted for Ballet Theatre in 1945.

For this we met in the studio of Edith Lutyens, the costumier, to discuss my costume. Chagall had asked Edith to make me a leotard of gold lamé, as there was no design, and he would then create the costume on me. Pieces of net in all colours were chosen and cut into feather-like shapes. With the leotard complete, I stood while Chagall used these fragments like paint, placing them on my body, at which moment Edith pinned them to the leotard.

My head-dress was designed by Chagall so that the Firebird's head and beak were on one side of my head, and they were, once again, made from bird of paradise feathers. My make-up was to be a dark body-wash on to which patches of grease were applied, and then gold-dust was scattered over my back, arms, shoulders, sticking to the grease, so that wherever I stood or moved the Firebird would gleam with extraordinary golden highlights. (I had to buy gold-dust by the pound when performances began; my dresser used to throw it on to my body.)

Ballet Theatre's management always tried to put *Firebird* last on the programme because it took so long to set and light, and my make-up was no less of a problem. After the performance it could not be wiped off, because the gold-dust was rough and scratched my skin badly. Thus I adopted the procedure of wearing a black cashmere sweater, which covered my arms and

# Marc Chagall, 'Aleko' and 'The Firebird'

back, after a performance so that I could dine with friends at curtain fall and then return to my apartment and soak off the wash and the gold in relative comfort. In big cities on tour I could do this in my hotel. But on short trips to smaller towns, and during the worst of the tours when we were obliged to travel by bus, there were times when I sat up all night in my Firebird make-up, or rushed to catch a 'plane without time to remove it—probably looking rather like Gary Glitter. After sitting up all night on a bus we might arrive at some High School auditorium for a performance in the afternoon and my first requirement was to find showers and a bathroom where I might cleanse myself of yesterday's gold-dust before getting ready for the opening ballet—*The Pas de Quatre* or *Princess Aurora*—and then having to don again the Firebird's colours and today's gilding for the final work in the programme. In later years Union ruling stipulated that artists who wore complex make-up should receive extra fees. Had that been the rule when I was dancing this *Firebird*, I should be a wealthy woman now.

Adolf Bolm, who staged *Firebird*, was the illustrious character dancer who so astounded Paris audiences as the Polovtsian Warrior Chief in *Prince Igor* on the first night of the first Diaghilev ballet season in 1909. He terrified the public then, but he was the soul of kindness, especially during tours, when both trains and meals were a constant worry. During one horrible journey in arctic weather through the Dakotas, I was suffering from a chill of nagging beastliness. I could not be left behind to recuperate in an hotel, so I travelled with the company, sitting in a compartment and feeling ready for death. I was sure I would never dance again. Suddenly Bolm entered the compartment laden with cans of baby food. He had bought them at the last train stop in a drug-store and these, he said, "would help me survive". Heated in boiling water they were instant easy nourishment, and thereafter I never travelled without such emergency rations.

Despite the fun and the comradeship and the undeniable hardships of these tours, travelling with the ballet was a very serious matter. We gave our life to the company, and there was no existence outside it, no thoughts of homes and mortgages and the worries attendant upon possessions. We were gypsies, and a mink coat was probably the extent of our treasure—and this a practical luxury because we needed to keep warm and were also expected to look glamorous.

Aleko *with Ballet Theatre, Mexico City, 1942. With Hugh Laing as the Gypsy Boy.*

*With George Skibine as Aleko in the opening scene and with Marc Chagall at the Metropolitan Opera House, New York, in 1967. Chagall was at the Met. to design* The Magic Flute.

*Adolf Bolm rehearsing us in his new
version of* The Firebird *for Ballet
Theatre, Hollywood, August 1945.*

*Rehearsing the first adagio with Pat Dolin.*

PHOTOGRAPH BY
CARL VAN VECHTEN

*Far left:* The Firebird *wearing the Chagall head-dress, 1945. New York.*
*Left: Chagall's Firebird in Carl van Vechten's studio. 1945. New York.*
*Below: With Carl van Vechten in New York, 1945.* "Carlo" *was a dear friend and advisor, as well as being a great photographer.*

IN 1942, DURING THE TIME THAT MIKHAIL FOKINE WAS working with Ballet Theatre, he wanted to stage *Romeo and Juliet* for me, with George Skibine as my Romeo. But when he heard the Prokofiev score—which had been suggested by Sol Hurok—Fokine turned it down. This was at a time when Ballet Theatre was spending a five-month period in Mexico City, performing at the Teatro Bellas Artes, and rehearsing and preparing the new ballets which would be shown during the forthcoming Met. season in New York and the subsequent coast to coast tour, with a further season at the Met. at the end of it.

During this period in Mexico, Fokine, Massine, Tudor and Dolin were all at work on new ballets, and I was involved in *Aleko* and *Don Domingo* with Massine, and *Romantic Age* with Dolin, while Fokine was creating his last ballet, *Helen of Troy*.

When Fokine rejected the Prokofiev score, it was offered to Antony Tudor, who also found it unsuitable. Antony then asked me if I would still like to be Juliet, and a week later invited me to dine with him and Hugh Laing and our conductor, Antal Dorati. Hugh and I were already at work on *Aleko*, and Antony had seen our partnership previously when I danced Caroline, with Hugh as her lover, in *Lilac Garden*. At dinner he told me that Dorati had come up with the idea of using music by Delius for *Romeo*; Ballet Theatre's management welcomed the proposal, and so the ballet went into rehearsal.

The first choice of designer was Salvador Dali, but his projected decors, though they may have been superb Dali, were unsuitable for *Romeo*: the balcony scene, I recall, was a set of giant false teeth supported by crutches! Happily, Eugene Berman was then invited to create the designs and these, inspired by Botticelli, were completely in harmony with Delius. (They were also marvellous: the great critic Edwin Denby hailed Berman's designs as "a serious work of art".)

Any spare time that I had from performances and other rehearsals was now spent working with Antony on *Romeo*. We continued to work on our return to the United States during Ballet Theatre's long coast-to-coast tour: I well remember rehearsing in many station waiting-rooms where we were marooned by war-time delays in the train schedules. We reached New York for the spring season at the Metropolitan Opera House, but *Romeo* was still not finished. My ideas about Juliet, how she felt and how she should look, were very clear to me. I knew that I did not want to wear my own black hair with the beautiful head-dresses that Berman had created. Instead, I thought that this young girl—who is only fourteen, albeit she

# Ballet Theatre 1942

# Sir Thomas Beecham and 'Romeo and Juliet'

grows to maturity within twenty-four hours—should have loose Botticellian red hair, as if the wind were blowing through it. And so my Juliet wore simple, loose russet hair.

On the first night the choreography was still incomplete. At the moment when Juliet takes the potion from Friar Lawrence, the great gold curtain fell. There followed four days of more than intense work. My life seemed entirely spent in moving between performances on the Met. stage and rehearsals in the studio on the top floor of the opera house. I even slept in my dressing-room. Once we worked all through the night, and I remember Sono Osato, who was the Rosaline, came into the rehearsal room in the morning bringing me orange juice and honey with vitamins. On another night Sol Hurok arrived just before five in the morning and took us all to Lindy's restaurant on Broadway and fed us smoked sturgeon, raw onion rings and rye bread. I then returned to my hotel at 7 a.m., and was back in the theatre for class and rehearsal two hours later.

Within four days the ballet was complete and scheduled for the Saturday night performance. I was also announced to appear in *Princess Aurora* at the matinee, but this was too much to ask of me; I withdrew and, as a result, Norah Kaye danced her first Aurora. I spent an hour of that matinee time driving in a cab round Central Park, breathing in the April air and looking at the trees, then returned to my hotel and slept the sleep of the very weary for a couple of hours, had a good meal, and danced Juliet in the complete ballet that night.

We had a most thrilling reception, but I had become very tired and as a result developed an eye infection. I rehearsed my repertory wearing a black eye-patch—which was an odd sight—but not so odd as the fact that I could not wear eye make-up on stage for several days. When I appeared as the dark-skinned gypsy girl Zemphira in *Aleko* one of my eyes was un-made-up. The effect for the audience was exactly as if I had a massive squint, and made me look not unlike Carmen Amaya.

*Romeo and Juliet* also became the occasion for very British evenings at the Met. when Sir Thomas Beecham was invited to conduct the Delius score. He had done an enormous amount to foster the public's understanding of this composer, and now we had two British dancers as Romeo and Juliet, in a ballet inspired by Shakespeare, by a British choreographer, danced to British music under Britain's greatest conductor. Beecham knew that Delius' music must be allowed to "breathe" and he adopted the correct concert tempi for the score, rather than the sometimes faster speeds that had been taken for our ballet performances. The music became so *sostenuto* that Hugh Laing used to mutter to me, "I'm going to die during these lifts," as he held me in his arms. One night Sir Thomas was particularly caught up in the music but, despite the slowness of the tempi, the music did not disintegrate. He had a supreme gift for sustaining its momentum, and the orchestra responded with superb playing. I was in seventh heaven at such inspired accompaniment. The stage management, however, was not. We had run fourteen minutes over time on this one ballet—and extra fees loomed for the musicians.

I had somewhat similar experiences with Beecham on two earlier occasions. In a Camargo Society performance in 1932 of Ninette de Valois' *Origin of Design,* in which I danced Terpsichore, Beecham came to conduct his arrangement of Handel's music, which was the ballet's score. At one point I finished a number supported in the air by two boys. We rehearsed with Beecham, who knew that after a pause the music should start again and the boys should lower me to the stage to continue the action. One night, after the applause that greeted this pose, I could see Beecham standing in the pit with his arms folded. The music did not continue. Consternation on stage. I whispered to the boys, whose arms were beginning to tremble with fatigue, "Put me down. You'd better kneel," and I adjusted myself to as pretty a pose as I could find between them. Then the music started up, the ballet went on, and we ended it in a state of puzzlement. After the performance Ninette came backstage, as curious as we were. Then Beecham appeared, mopping himself, and after congratulating us on "keeping our heads", he admitted that he had thought, "That's a very pretty group when they hold Alicia up there," and had decided that the audience should be allowed to enjoy it a little longer before continuing with the ballet.

On another occasion he played a trick at a different speed on me. He was conducting *Façade* (for the first and only time) on the closing night of the Camargo Society season at the Savoy Theatre in 1932. He admired Walton's music very much and had watched our performances, so that he knew the exact tempi we needed. Before the performance Constant Lambert, who habitually conducted this score for us, said to me, "I wish you luck," and *Façade* began. All went well until my Polka. At first the speed was perfectly correct, but at the return of the refrain Sir Thomas started to accelerate. I have always followed the music, and so I kept up with him, knowing that there was a double *tour en l'air* to be fitted in (a step which has now been lost from the ballet). Everything went well. We finished together, and during the applause I could see Sir Thomas grinning at me. Afterwards he came backstage and said to me, "Well, how was it?" All I could say was that it had been a joy working with him ... but hadn't the Polka ended rather faster than usual? "Yes, my dear, I meant it to. I've been watching you. You have great speed, and I wanted to know just how fast you could go. So I went for it and, good girl, you kept up with me. Oh, that *was* exciting! Good girl!"

The good girl remembered the incident ten years later, during the inspired tempi for *Romeo* in New York.

*With Ballet Theatre in Mexico City, 1942, leaving the stage door of the Teatro Bellas Artes with Antony Tudor and Hugh Laing, on our way to dinner and discussions for* Romeo and Juliet.

*Right and following pages: Antony Tudor's* Romeo and Juliet *for Ballet Theatre, with design by Eugene Berman. Hugh Laing as Romeo, Nicholas Orlov as the dead Mercutio and Richard Reed as Paris.*

DURING MY SECOND SEASON WITH BALLET THEATRE, I HAD, as was usual at that time, been over-working. During a rehearsal of Massine's *Mam'zelle Angot,* in which I was to create the role of the Aristocrat with André Eglevsky as the Caricaturist, I had been set some acrobatic steps to perform of the kind which Massine loved to give me, and I fainted from a sudden wrenched muscle in my side. I contrived to appear that night in the performance of *Aleko* at the Hollywood Bowl, and towards the end of the ballet I collapsed in full view of the capacity audience of 35,000 people.

Hugh Laing, my partner, carried me off stage, and Muriel Bentley dashed on for the closing moments of the ballet so that Aleko might have someone to stab at the climax of the action. Meantime I had been taken in agony to my hotel. The pain was not appendicitis, as I had thought. I was diagnosed as having "pulled a muscle", strapped in plaster, and left behind in Hollywood as the company took off for the rest of its tour. After a few days during which La Argentinita and her sister, Pilar Lopez, angelically helped look after me, I returned to New York to dance in the opening performance of the Ballet Theatre season at the Met. Pat Dolin was partnering me in the second act of *Swan Lake* when, during the lifts in the great *adagio,* I again nearly fainted from pain as his hands gripped my waist for the supported work.

I went forthwith to consult a great émigré Viennese doctor, who diagnosed a hernia. An operation was essential. The chance of my being able to dance afterwards was thought to be remote by everyone, except this outstanding surgeon. And me. I had implicit faith in him.

After the operation complete rest was essential, and I was confined to my hotel room, living on the attentions of room service and the visits of friends such as Vincenzo Celli, my coach, and of a few dancers, led by John Taras, who used to come in the evenings and bring food and wine for picnics in my room. (It was Celli who also brought me a kitten that Maestro Toscanini, a friend of his, sent me as a "get well" gift. Bambi, the kitten, was a great joy during three months of enforced rest and unaccustomed inaction.)

Pat Dolin telephoned me each evening at 11 p.m. after curtain down on Ballet Theatre's performance, from whatever city the company happened to be playing in, to report on the day's activities and to urge me back to work as quickly as possible. I welcomed these contacts since I felt miserable at being left behind, and very worried about my financial situation. I planned to rejoin the company in January, and just before this,

*With my friend and coach Vincenzo Celli, New York, 1942.*

Agnes de Mille called to see me, telling me she had seen the impresario Billy Rose and his wife, Eleanor Holm, at the theatre on the previous evening. Billy was planning a new spectacular show, to be called *The Seven Lively Arts*. Agnes continued, "Billy asked me who was the greatest dancer in the world. I said you were, and so if you get a 'phone call from him, you'll know how and why!"

I was soon to meet Billy, who was bursting with ideas for the show. Of course, the news of our being seen together reached the gossip columns in the newspapers, who made various guesses that I was to be engaged for the forthcoming production, but I was shocked and amazed to receive an injunction from Ballet Theatre expressly forbidding me from appearing in Billy's projected revue, since I had made no decision to do so.

My lawyers fought the injunction and took my case to arbitration, where note was taken of my previously very heavy performance schedule with Ballet Theatre and of the fact that I had every intention of appearing with the company as soon as I could. The case was swiftly concluded in my favour. As soon as I was fit, I went out on tour with Ballet Theatre, able only to dance *Romeo and Juliet,* but eager to get on stage again. While we were touring Billy perpetrated a splendid "tease" on the management by telephoning me each evening near curtain time, so that the back-stage rang with the stage manager's shouts of, "Long distance call for Miss Markova." "Mr Rose calling from New York for Miss Markova." All Billy ever said on the 'phone was, "How are you, honey? Eleanor sends love. Keep well. This is just to make them Goddammed *mad*!" Which it did.

By the end of the Ballet Theatre tour I knew that it would be hard for me to sustain the gruelling routine that performances would pile on top of the difficulties of travelling through war-time America. Thus, I agreed that, in the late autumn of 1943, I would appear in *The Seven Lively Arts* with Pat Dolin as my partner. The idea of the revue was to feature outstanding artists in theatre, dance, music, painting, comedy. Billy Rose had even gone to the trouble of buying the old Ziegfeld Theatre and restoring it entirely, so that there were murals by Dali. Dorothy Hammerstein had been entrusted with the interior decoration of the artists' quarters. These were opulent. The stars of the show—Beatrice Lillie; Bert Lahr; Benny Goodman; Pat and me—were given a dressing-room, bathroom, costume-room, each on one floor of the theatre. Bea was on the first floor; then came Bert; above him was my suite; then Benny's; then Pat's;

and above us the other members of the cast. Dorothy Hammerstein had designed our quarters as "typical"; hence the doors to our apartments were painted with the emblems of our art rather than our names. Bea had a big bumblebee; Bert had an axe, as a reminder of his woodsman sketch; Benny had a clarinet; Pat and I had the shoes of our calling, and my rooms were also decorated in white *broderie anglaise,* with pink walls. All this was, furthermore, a surprise gift to us; we knew nothing of it until we moved into the theatre.

In discussing the show, Billy Rose had asked me, "Who's the greatest living composer?" I had promptly replied, "Igor Stravinsky." And Billy forthwith set about commissioning a score from him. This was to be *Scènes de ballet,* and during the Ballet Theatre tour and a further Hollywood Bowl season, Pat and I were able to see Stravinsky in Hollywood, where he was then living, and renew acquaintance with him and his wife, Vera. We spent happy afternoons lunching and chatting, usually about the news or the incidents in the radio programmes we all listened to, but also, of course, discussing the score as it progressed, and the sort of ballet it would be. The score which Stravinsky eventually produced was the masterpiece we know today, and I am most proud that it should have been created for me, at my suggestion. The ballet which we choreographed was a classical work, and it opened the second half of the show. My first entrance, I vividly remember, was a tremendous run down a long ramp that was part of Norman Bel Geddes' great setting: the impression as I raced down, past the ice-blue and white backdrop, was exactly that of looking out of an aeroplane window on to a cloud-dotted blue sky.

The rest of the music in the show was by Cole Porter. I went to see him in his New York apartment at the Waldorf Towers, to discuss a score for our second appearance in the revue. Cole suggested that we use one of his songs for a *pas de deux.* He proposed *Night and Day,* but I felt that this was too well-known and, as he began playing some of his other music, Cole remembered that there was a symphonic version of *Easy to Love* which had been orchestrated for a Hollywood musical, but never used. Based exactly on the pattern of the Ponchielli Dance of the Hours from *La Gioconda* (which I remembered from Fred Ashton's version that I had danced a decade before at the Regal Cinema, in London) this was re-orchestrated for the show by Robert Russell Bennett, and Pat and I choreographed it jointly.

*The Seven Lively Arts* had a try-out in Philadelphia at the end of November and, after two weeks running the show in, we

*The finale of* Seven Lively Arts.

brought it to New York in early December. Thereafter we played it twice nightly until the following May. During the run of the show I used to warm-up for performance in the vestibule outside my dressing-room, using the balustrade of the staircase as a barre, since I had the whole of my floor of the theatre to myself and I could work undisturbed. One day the doors of the lift which connected our dressing-rooms to the stage opened, and Benny Goodman looked out in some amazement and asked me what I was doing. I told him I always warmed-up during the first half of the show before *Scènes de ballet*. "I tune up too," he said with a laugh and, because I was working without music, he suggested that we should tune-up together. For the next few weeks we did just that. In the show Benny had to play the jazz which his public expected of him, but during our barre sessions he played Mozart while I worked on *pliés* and *tendus*. People suggested that this might have been put into the show, with Benny playing as I worked in practice clothes, but the idea was not practicable, and our private warm-up sessions remained marvellous but intensely personal, as we got ready for our public.

And even though we were giving twelve performances a week, Pat and I contrived to make some Sunday night appearances at the Met. with Ballet Theatre, where I danced *The Pas de Quatre* and *Romeo and Juliet*. On other Sunday evenings it was also customary to appear for the Theatre Benevolent Fund and, whenever possible, to dance at the Stage Door Canteen as well. We were not idle.

# Touring, Revolutions and a trip to the Philippines 1945-48

IN THE YEARS IMMEDIATELY FOLLOWING *The Seven Lively Arts* Pat Dolin and I seemed to be dancing in an extraordinary range of theatres, with different companies, in concert performances, and with our own Markova-Dolin Company. We were guesting once again with Ballet Theatre, and while touring with them we initiated our group of twelve dancers, headed by Rosella Hightower and George Skibine, with whom we could perform in those smaller centres which Ballet Theatre was unable to visit. It meant a complex schedule, the juggling of two repertories which I danced, and also much travel as missionaries of ballet.

I can recall leaving Ballet Theatre performances, where I had just ended the evening's programme as the Firebird, and, still in full gold-dust and brown stage make-up, racing to a 'plane for a quick flight, and only being able to wash off this war-paint after our arrival at some small town where we were to dance with our group the next day. This routine continued until Sol Hurok, who was now our personal manager, parted company with Ballet Theatre and decided to present the de Basil Original Ballet Russe, which had somehow managed to weather the war years in South America. Now Hurok brought de Basil's company to New York and invited Pat and me to lead them, with the inducement for me of a new production of ,*Camille* that John Taras was to choreograph to Schubert music, with ravishing designs by Cecil Beaton sponsored by Elizabeth Arden.

With our own Markova-Dolin Ballet we also undertook the first ever tour of the Caribbean states, visiting Cuba, El Salvador, Venezuela, Guatemala, Costa Rica, and other islands. The trip was arduous, not least because we were travelling by air—the first ballet company to do so on a tour—playing to audiences that had sometimes never seen ballet. An added hazard was the political instability of the region. Revolutions seemed part of the way of life. (Matinée and evening performances were cancelled in Bogotà, Colombia, during which we were advised by the British Consulate to stay in our hotel because "there is going to be shooting today". I was not sorry about this because of the problems that altitude causes any dancer.) On our island-hopping Pan-Am flights we got to know pilots and crew, and they were kind enough to bring us the Miami newspapers whenever possible so as to keep us in touch with events. They also brought us fresh milk: the local milk was not to be drunk if one valued one's health. We were supposed, one day, to make a brief stop-over in Nicaragua to lunch with Alice Delysia, an old friend of Pat, who lived there

*With Anton Dolin and Sol Hurok, 1944.*

with her husband, a French colonial official. Our pilot declared, though, in an unforgettable phrase, "I can't put you down. They're revolting. They're always doing it, and this time they've taken the airport." So we missed luncheon and the possibility of a bullet in the hors d'œuvre.

In the summer of 1947 Pat and I also made an extended visit to Mexico, helping to launch a national ballet there, then returned to New York for a brief season at the Met. with our own company, before another coast-to-coast tour. Our next journey was even more taxing.

We were invited to perform in the Philippines in a solo programme, with a pianist. My sister Doris (who was now our stage manager) and Alfred Katz (our manager) were the only other members of our party. This trip was to precede our return to England as guests at Covent Garden in the spring of 1948, and I did not realize that before the tour was over my weight would be reduced by the tropical heat of the Philippines to eighty-five pounds—dancing in a temperature of over 100 degrees is better than any steam room for slimming.

Our journey to Manila was long, but not uneventful. After performing in San Francisco, we took a 'plane for Hawaii—virgin territory for ballet—where the heat and humidity were such that my ballet shoes no longer fitted. I managed somehow to dance, but made urgent calls to Capezio, my New York shoe-maker, to order "tropical" shoes which were a size larger and more strongly blocked than the very light shoes I always wore. (In the humidity of the Pacific my usual point shoes were reduced to pulp within minutes.) From Honolulu to Manila was a four-day flight, with re-fuelling stops on the American military bases at Wake Island and Guam, where I was able to get hot tea to drink. If I was to survive this journey I knew that I had to sleep—I have the priceless gift of being able to sleep on journeys of all kinds—and a mattress was installed on the floor of our 'plane so that I could stretch out and rest completely for much of the flight. Our diet for the journey was cold roast chicken and salad: delicious, but slightly monotonous after the first day.

Eventually we reached Manila, a town largely reduced to rubble by war-time bombing, with our hotel itself a victim, since only half of it was standing. (I remember opening a door next to my suite, which led directly and terrifyingly on to nothingness: the rest of the building had been sheared away by bombing.) The population seemed military in the main, and at the hotel check-in desk was a notice: *Park your Fire-Arms Here*, necessitated, I was told, by a shoot-out the day before.

Camille, *choreographed by John Taras, and designed by Cecil Beaton, for the Original Ballet Russe in 1946.*

*Left: Being greeted by Cecil Beaton at Dublin Airport, 1959. I was making a guest appearance with Festival Ballet at the Dublin Festival, and was to dance my first, and last, Giselle in Ireland. This was to be my final appearance in my favourite ballet.*

The town was devastating to see, with streets merely marked by long chains of petrol cans strung together. Our first appearance was delayed by the sudden death of the President, and national mourning meant that theatrical performances were impossible. Thus we embarked upon an instant tour of the islands in a converted military 'plane with desperately uncomfortable bucket seats made all the more unwelcoming by the blistering 120 degree temperature—you could be toasted as you sat in them wearing only thin cotton clothing. From the air there seemed nothing at all in the island of Cebu where we were scheduled to dance. But as we landed we discovered that an audience drove in from miles around to watch us in our appearance in an open-air cinema, which was the only possible theatre there. Scenery, of course, was non-existent, but I have vividly in mind the sight of dozens of Filipino women sitting on the ground, sewing together opened-out military sacks and then stitching masses of tuberoses on to them so that we might have a back-drop to our performance, while on either side of the stage were gasoline drums also packed with tuberoses. The scent was almost overpowering, and so was the warmth of the reception we received, which made all the discomfort and inadequacies seem no price to pay for being able to bring something to these generous and delightful people who had lost everything during the Japanese occupation.

On our return to Manila we were able to perform, though there seemed to be only one piano on the island which it was possible to use for our shows. At the end of our visit we realized that many Filipinos had not been able to see us, and we decided to give one final performance at which the ticket price would be one dollar, so that as many people as possible might enjoy a ballet performance for the first time, provided that we could find a location large enough. This turned out to be the local baseball stadium, still miraculously intact after the war-time raids. A symphony orchestra was re-assembled, and part of the purpose of the show was that they should receive the proceeds of the evening to enable them to buy much-needed new instruments. Something like a boxing ring was adopted to provide a stage. Lighting was found for us by the U.S. Army, who loaned searchlights. My sister Doris had a difficult task in arranging for the necessary gelatines to be taped over the lamps to create a proper stage illusion. The power for the lighting was obtained by running electric cables through the city to the stadium. Manila was told that there would be no electricity in the town from 6 p.m. onwards, so that our performance might be visible. (I have the impression, though, that there were no people at home in Manila that night to bother about any absence of illumination: they were all at the stadium.)

We danced in this extraordinary and extraordinarily moving setting, and I can recall few performances that made me prouder of being able to share the art of ballet with the public.

# A Cuban Stage

THE WORST STAGE I HAVE EVER DANCED ON WAS IN CUBA, WHEN Pat Dolin and I were touring there during the late 1940s. We went with our pianist to give concert performances, but when we arrived at the theatre we discovered a stage so warped by heat and damp that it was absolutely corrugated. How to dance on it? We managed to negotiate its ridges for part of the evening, and for the first and only time in my life I danced that *Sylphides* prelude off point, picking my way across the bumps, while Pat managed the same feat for his solos. But *The Dying Swan* must be performed with a rippling *pas de bourrée* on point. We asked the management if they could possibly find a piece of linoleum to lay down before my swan must die: it might otherwise have died from a broken ankle. Before too long the stage manager arrived with the linoleum and a crew of men with hammers. They laid the lino in full view of the public, to the accompaniment of the audience's singing, and eventually I was able to pick my way through the dance, bourréeing up and down hill over the bumpy stage.

*Overleaf: With Jerome Robbins, André Eglevsky, Anton Dolin, rehearsing for the Robbins/Berlioz* Pas de trois *with the Original Ballet Russe, 1947.*

# RETURN
# TO EUROPE
# 1948-62

# Return to London and Retirement 1948-63

AFTER A DECADE AWAY FROM MY HOMELAND, I RETURNED TO England in 1948, when Pat Dolin and I were invited to appear as guests with the Sadler's Wells Ballet at Covent Garden.

Pat decided to fly the Atlantic. I knew that six days of shipboard peace and quiet would help me to start recuperating from our Philippine performances, and I disappeared from view to my state-room for the entire journey. It had been intended that two weeks should elapse after our arrival before we appeared in *Giselle,* but a panic call from London urged us to appear at the Ballet's Benevolent Fund Gala, a day after our return. Thus I appeared in London in the *Don Quixote pas de deux* on sea-legs, Covent Garden's stage still rearing up towards me like the deck of the *Queen Elizabeth.* Thereafter we were to renew acquaintance with many old friends and with the classic repertory I had known in the earliest days of our national ballet: *Giselle* and *Swan Lake.* I was also able to make my début in the full-length *Sleeping Beauty*—my six-day sleep on the boat a preparation for Aurora's hundred year siesta—which brought an exceptional wave of memories for me of the *Sleeping Princess* which I had seen at the Alhambra Theatre in 1921, accompanied by Diaghilev.

The ensuing year meant a great deal of commuting between America and Britain: in the space of one week I appeared at Covent Garden, Madison Square Gardens, New York, and the Hollywood Bowl. As these last two locations indicate, Pat and I had become pioneers of "arena ballet". In London we were to dance at the Empress Hall and at Harringey, while in Montreal we appeared in a baseball stadium where I was escorted out on to the stage by a contingent of Mounties. We also continued our world tours, going back to the Caribbean and making a first visit to Kenya, Rhodesia and South Africa. On this tour we also flew to Lourenço Marques (in the then Mozambique) to give a recital. This we shared with our pianist, Leon Kuschner, who played while we were changing from one number to the next. For his solos, the piano was rolled to the centre of the stage, and in Lourenço Marques the stage proved so rotten that a leg of the piano went right through the boards, leaving a hole which Pat and I spent the rest of the evening circumnavigating as best we could. After the performance there came profuse apologies from the management. I suggested that, for the sake of future visiting artists, they promise to have the stage repaired as soon as possible. The manager agreed, but added, "we don't know when that will be." It turned out that the artist who had last appeared on that stage before us was Anna Pavlova in 1924!

*Previous page: A studio portrait by Baron, London 1956.*

Giselle *at the Royal Opera House, Covent Garden, in 1948: with Dolin in the first act.*

Swan Lake *Act Three, with the Sadler's Wells Ballet, when Pat and I returned as guests to Covent Garden in 1948.*

*The beautiful, melancholy variation* Autumn, *choreographed for me by dear Bronislava Nijinska to Tchaikovsky music in 1948.*

We had been invited to Africa for a four-week season, but we were encouraged to extend our stay to three months, although the beginning of the trip was marked for me by the great shock and grief of my mother's death. Somehow, I contrived to finish the tour.

Once back in London there came a further invitation to tour, this time round Britain with Gala Performances of Ballet. Under the management of Julian Braunsweg, we had the support of a corps de ballet and some gifted soloists from the Arts Educational School, who were to form the embryo of the next company we founded: Festival Ballet. Launched in 1950, Festival Ballet made a first provincial tour which I had to miss because of an operation for appendicitis, but I felt that the company was especially mine in that I had christened it—a tribute to the Festival of Britain which was held in that year.

By the autumn of 1950 Festival Ballet had come to London for a first season at the Stoll Theatre, and within a year it was firmly established. We presented the nineteenth century classics, masterpieces of twentieth century ballet, and also a more personal repertory, and we invited many of the most eminent names in the world of ballet to be our guests. It was

*An advertisement for the first London season by Festival Ballet, 1950.*

a joy to be reunited with Choura Danilova and Leonid Massine, and to present such artists as Yvette Chauviré, Mia Slavenska, Tatiana Riabouchinska and David Lichine, Milorad Miskovich, as well as our resident ballerina Natalie Krassovska, and John Gilpin, our young *premier danseur*.

But after two years of unremitting work to establish the company, an injury forced me to rest and on my return to dancing I felt that I needed more freedom to accept the myriad invitations which flooded in to me to dance throughout the world. So, while Pat remained with Festival Ballet, I was to dance as internationally as I ever had done before: appearing as a guest throughout Europe and the Americas, with Ballet Theatre, the Royal Danish Ballet, the Grand Ballet du Marquis de Cuevas, the Festival Ballet, both halves of The Royal Ballet. I also found myself back on Broadway with the Chicago Ballet in *The Merry Widow,* and in a work based on *Il trovatore*—Ruth Page's *Revanche*. I danced in an Italian opera season at Drury Lane in London; appeared with the eminent Indian dancer Ram Gopal in London and at the Edinburgh Festival; made guest appearances with Pilar Lopez and her company in Spain, and toured in concert performances with Milorad Miskovich. This recital programme took a year to construct, and we performed it in Britain and then took it to Paris, Italy (where we appeared at the Nervi Festival) and the United States, at the vast open-air auditorium of the Greek Theatre in Hollywood. I danced again in Cuba, at the time when Fidel Castro was preparing his revolution, and was a little alarmed by the evening broadcasts from his rebel radio station in the hills which announced, "Tonight we shall take Havana!" He did not accomplish this while I was there.

I also made a memorable visit to the Teatro Colòn, Buenos Aires. I had been invited to dance in a new staging of *Swan Lake* and, with my partner Roman Jasinsky, to give my concert performances. I was on the point of leaving New York for Buenos Aires when the news came of the death of Evita Peron, and we were advised to delay our departure for two weeks because of national mourning. Quite how intense this was to be did not occur to me until our arrival in Buenos Aires, when, before passing through customs and immigration, we were shepherded into a temporary chapel, massed with flowers, where we were required to pay our respects to "The Lady". Next day I was taken to the theatre to meet the management and the dancers, and I was led through the stage door straight into another temporary chapel, replete with flowers and a large portrait of "The Lady". (One paid one's respects each time one passed—either in or out—through the stage door.)

During rehearsals a few days later the orchestral sound appeared a little thin. My conductor, Robert Zeller, said to me, "Don't worry. Only two thirds of the musicians are here, but they will all be rehearsed and present for the performance!" It seemed that each day numbers of musicians were away, playing for the Requiem Masses held for the last repose of "The Lady".

On the opening night of *Swan Lake* I was thrilled to receive a mountain of flowers, which were eventually brought to my dressing-room. I noticed with some alarm that my dresser, Maria, was suddenly making a bee-line for the door, laden with an armful of flowers. These were "For the Lady! For The Lady!" I was told that a quota of all one's flowers were taken to the stage door chapel. Beyond insisting that at least I be left with the cards so that I would know whom to thank, I could only agree to this tax.

Nor was this all. At a rehearsal on the day before my last performance, I said to the stage manager, "I'll see you tomorrow night," to which there came the reply, "No. *Morning.* Tomorrow morning. Nine o'clock. Syndicate!" It seemed that I, like every other visiting artist, must give an early morning performance for the trades unions. Early next day—morning is absolutely my worst time of day—a rapt and attentive audience crowded the Teatro Colòn and I gave the earliest performance of my career. I would have been happier to dance for the unions rather later—and certainly not on the morning of my farewell performance in Buenos Aires.

The years and the performances raced past. On 1 January 1963 I was at Heathrow Airport on my way to New York. As usual, a group of pressmen were at the airport to talk to me before my flight. I had recently recovered from a particularly nasty tonsil operation, and I was concerned to get myself back into training after my illness, and I was still wondering, as inevitably one must, what roles I should next undertake, and how best to use my energies after a holiday in the sun to recuperate.

A newsman suddenly asked me, "Do you have any New Year Resolutions?" Suddenly, and without premeditation, I replied, "Yes. I don't think I shall ever dance in public again." I spoke, it now seems to me, without thinking. I had not discussed this decision with anyone, but in my fifty-second year, I felt it the right thing to do. I needed to use my energies differently.

The news made the headlines worldwide that day. By the time the 'plane took off for New York, the die was cast.

Italian Suite *pas de deux, in performance with Dolin at the Empress Hall, London, in 1949.*

The *"Snowflakes" scene from* The Nutcracker, *with Dolin and the corps de ballet at the Empress Hall, London, in 1949.*

Backstage with Festival Ballet in 1951, with my dear and devoted Edna Barnard, my dresser and friend for many years.

In 1953 I returned as guest to the Sadler's Wells Ballet at Covent Garden.

# Television

I WAS AMONG THE FIRST DANCERS TO APPEAR ON TELEVISION. Long before there were regular broadcasts, John Logie Baird was making experimental transmissions in 1932, and he invited me to appear in some of them.

The difficulties under which we worked were bizarre in the extreme. In my earliest performance I danced to a piano solo and had to disappear from camera view by creeping under the piano when my dance was finished. This experiment took place in a little room in Portland Place, London, the floor covered with black and white squares, while the camera produced a flickering beam of illumination rather like strobe-lighting—all this crammed into an area not more than twelve feet square. Costumes had to be outlined with black ribbon to increase their visibility, and my first make-up for the camera was a dead white face with black lips and purple eye-shadow to increase *my* visibility. Later, with the BBC, there followed further experimentation, and something called "panchromatic" make-up was evolved—my face and lips had to be brick-red and rust coloured. Even odder was the fact that these transmissions could only be seen in a few locations which had special receiving sets: I recall that Selfridge's Store in Oxford Street was one, and advertisements in the newspapers announced that the public could see them there.

Later I moved to Alexandra Palace to take part in early BBC television programmes, where I used to dance accompanied by the eminent pianist Mark Hambourg. Eventually we graduated to using an orchestra, but this meant a terrible crowd in the studio, and the next development brought the separation of music and dance. The ever-reliable Eric Robinson (with whom I was to work a great deal later on in television) and his orchestra were placed in one studio and I danced simultaneously in another. There were no monitor screens, and a call-boy was employed to run between the studios to let the musicians know when I was ready to dance and to tell me when they were to start playing. Confusing though this may sound, we achieved a great deal, and I gave my last pre-war TV performance at Alexandra Palace in 1939, just before hostilities ended television transmissions.

In New York Pat Dolin and I danced in the first pioneering transmissions by NBC, performing *Giselle* in a 'dry-run' experiment, with Martinelli as representative of opera. After the war huge technical progress had been made, and I was involved in numberless television shows in New York and London. Alas, recording of performances was not usual in those days, since we appeared live. With the last shot the dance was lost forever.

*On Good Friday 1953, the BBC presented a very special production of* Les Sylphides *for television. Left to right: Lydia Sokolova, who staged and rehearsed the corps de ballet; Cyril Beaumont, who advised on the staging; Svetlana Beriosova; Tamara Karsavina, who talked about the original production in which she had danced; the producer Christian Simpson; myself; and Violetta Elvin.*

I am sad to think of some of the wonderful programmes that are gone beyond recall. These include Max Liberman's *Show of Shows,* the biggest Saturday night entertainment, coast to coast, on American TV, presented by NBC. It starred Imogene Coca and Sid Caesar, and was written by Mel Brooks, Woody Allen and Carl Reiner. Transmitted live, it allowed me to bring my dancing into millions of homes for the first time, and also found me as mistress of ceremonies, introducing the show— without the benefit of cue cards. Thank heavens for a good memory!

There was also a memorable *Les Sylphides* for the BBC which was supervised by Tamara Karsavina, Lydia Sokolova and Cyril Beaumont, in which I danced with Svetlana Beriosova, Violetta Elvin and John Field. And a *Giselle* with Erik Bruhn, shot soon after our New York performances, in which we were supported by Ballet Rambert.

A few shows have survived, and the Museum of Television in New York preserves some programmes from among the many early NBC transmissions in which I appeared.

*Above left: As the Sugar Plum Fairy in Festival Ballet's* The Nutcracker *at the Stoll Theatre in 1950.*

*Above: The Snowflakes scene from* The Nutcracker *for television's* Sunday Night at The Palladium *in 1957.*

*Coaching four of Festival Ballet's Sugar Plum Fairies: Belinda Wright, Olga Ferri, Dianne Richards, Marilyn Burr.*

The Pas de Quatre *with Festival Ballet: Riabouchinska, Markova, Danilova, Krassovska.*

Bolero 1830 *created for me by Ana Ricarda in 1953 for my concert programme.*

Les Sylphides *with George Skibine and the Grand Ballet du Marquis de Cuevas, Théâtre de l'Empire, Paris, 1953.*

*Bournonville's* La Sylphide *with Serge Golovine, in the staging for the Grand Ballet du Marquis de Cuevas at the Théâtre des Champs Elysées, Paris, in 1955. The role of the Sylphide was taught me by my friend Hans Brenaa, the leading Bournonville authority, and was a great favourite of mine.*

The Dying Swan. *Rio de Janeiro, 1956.*

Aurora's Wedding *with Oleg Briansky. An action photo taken from the wings in Rio de Janeiro, 1956.*

*Opposite: Portrait by Dorothy Wilding, New York, 1955.*

*At the Albert Hall in 1954, after a concert performance of The Sugar Plum Fairy solo from* The Nutcracker.

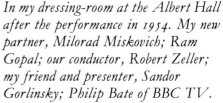

*In my dressing-room at the Albert Hall after the performance in 1954. My new partner, Milorad Miskovich; Ram Gopal; our conductor, Robert Zeller; my friend and presenter, Sandor Gorlinsky; Philip Bate of BBC TV.*

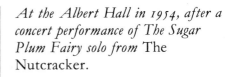

Orfeo *at the Metropolitan Opera House, New York 1955. The Blessed Spirit.*

*In my dressing-room at the Met., with Rudolf Bing.*

Orfeo, *Metropolitan Opera House,*
*New York, 1955. The Blessed Spirit.*

L'Après-midi d'un faune, *New*
*York, 1954.*

# About 'Giselle'

PHOTOGRAPHS OF *Giselle* IN PERFORMANCE CAN SOMETIMES capture a great deal about the charm and drama and other-worldly serenities of this great ballet. What, fortunately, photographs do not capture, are the dramas and far from serene moments which happen back-stage before, and sometimes during, performance. I have memories, hilarious and fraught, about performance, ranging from coping with drunks to coping with death-threats and even coping with the scenery.

Preparing oneself for the role of Giselle demands concentration, especially when the mad scene and death which end the first act have to be followed by a change of costume and make-up and temperamental feeling to prepare for the sublimities of the second act, when Giselle is an all-forgiving spirit. I found this very difficult one night in Canada, when I returned to my dressing-room to discover that a member of the Ballet Russe de Monte Carlo had decided to end an emotional crisis in her life by taking to the vodka bottle. She lay— far gone in drink, remorse and terrible disarray—in the bathroom we had to use, and my preparation for the second act was more than a little delayed and disorganized, as we tried to bring her round with smelling salts, black coffee and any other aids to sobriety and good sense we could find. The second act curtain was held, but eventually I was able to get back on stage to appear as the tranquil and protective Wili Giselle, having gone through not only the crisis of the mad-scene on stage, but a no less mad scene back-stage.

The worst Giselle drama, though, preceded my New York début as Giselle in 1938, with the Ballet Russe de Monte Carlo. Leonid Massine had decided I should open the season, with Serge Lifar as my Albrecht. The priority of performances was immaterial to me. I was confident that Giselle was a role in which I gave of my best, and public acclaim and the enthusiasm of European critics had taught me that it was a ballet in which I was admired. More important, it was a ballet in which I found continuing riches of emotion and dance to explore: it was always fresh for me throughout my career, as I stepped out of the cottage in Act One. So, had Toumanova or Slavenska, who had danced their first Giselles in London during our Drury Lane season, been given the New York première at the Met., I should not have felt too deflated. However Massine and Sol Hurok were insistent that I should dance the opening performance, and that Lifar should partner me, although I had already surmised that he would have preferred to appear with the beautiful Toumanova.

When we arrived in New York, Serge Lifar, who was a guest artist, demanded once again that Toumanova should dance the opening performance. Leonid Massine and Hurok refused, point blank, arguing that my reputation had preceded me and the company, and that I was now the accepted choice for the role, and that New York audiences were already anticipating my American debut in an interpretation of which they had heard much from European reports. On the day preceding the first performance, we were rehearsing *Seventh Symphony* in the Met. studio, when Toumanova's father appeared and, in the middle of rehearsal, when we had broken for a moment, approached Massine and asked if his daughter was dancing Giselle on the following night. Massine told him, "No. Markova will be dancing." At this moment Papa Toumanova slapped Massine's face. Unruffled, Massine simply clapped his hands and the rehearsal proceeded.

In due time I went back to the dressing-room I shared with Choura Danilova, to change. That evening it had been planned that Choura and I, with Freddie Franklin and Igor Youskevich, should go and see the Rodeo at Madison Square Gardens, as a relaxing outing before the excitements of the opening night of the season. We had been given a box: we were guests of the Rodeo, and a certain amount of publicity had been organized as a result. Choura and I stood at the stage door of the Met., waiting for a taxi and watching the rush-hour crowd surge past on 40th Street. There was a good deal of jostling and pushing as the commuters hurried by, and someone bumped into me. Before I realized it, a piece of paper had been pushed into my hand. At this moment our cab arrived and, as Choura and I settled into it to go back to our hotel, I realized that I was still clutching the paper. Looking at it I saw that there was a message on it for me. *Don't dance Giselle tomorrow night, or ...*

I suddenly felt very shaken. As soon as we reached our hotel, Choura insisted that I go to her room, and from there she contacted Hurok. Hurok's office rallied at once, and we were told to spend the evening as planned. I would then stay with Choura in her suite, and she would remain with me. To make sure that no mishap occurred, Hurok advised us that "people from the office" would be around us to make sure that no trouble arose, and that on the morrow I would have a bodyguard, but his presence would be known to no one save Choura and myself. The evening passed pleasantly. The following morning everyone back-stage at the Met. found themselves issued with passes, and a rule established that without a pass there was no admittance.

We rehearsed the production with a walk-through that morning, and I knew that I had the inestimable comfort of Choura with me on stage in Act Two, as Myrtha, Queen of the Wilis, and off-stage as a protecting friend. After a rest at my hotel, I returned to the Met. for my American début—a matter of great importance for me and for the Ballet Russe de Monte Carlo.

I was not able, though, to make all my usual careful preparations with which I always preceded a performance. We had originally rehearsed with trap-doors to allow Giselle to appear and disappear in the second act. Now Massine ordered, "No traps," for fear of some mishap to me. These charming devices were dispensed with, and instead, I took the stage at curtain-up with security men positioned in each wing, watching me like hawks. And as if this were not enough of a strain on my first-night nerves, there came an additional hazard in Act Two.

Serge Lifar had the caprice that he must bring real Easter lilies to Giselle's tomb. His entrance, holding them in a cascade from his arms, was always very beautiful at the start of Act Two. But if you tread on a lily it tends to become squelchy. Lifar strewed them across the stage. For the rest of the act, the corps de ballet of Wilis and I spent our time desperately trying to avoid them. The corps slipped and skidded, one after another. The floor-patterns for the Wilis' dances could not allow them to move clear. I was able to avoid the lilies (though at what extra expense of nervous energy!) as I tried to negotiate patches of green slime, and dance my best, and also develop a protective and loving interpretation with the perpetrator of this vegetable mess.

I picked my way through them, but the carpet of flattened lilies played havoc with the corps de ballet, for just as they were making a leap, they would see a patch of green slipperiness in their path and evasive action had to be taken to avoid a serious fall. As if this were not enough—security men; slimy lily stems; stupid intrigues—there came yet another floral incident. In this production Giselle, as a Wili, had to pluck lilies from the ground row at the back of the stage to throw to Albrecht from the height of a jump. It is one of the loveliest images in this lovely ballet, as the soaring Giselle tosses a flower behind her at the peak of a diagonal leap. In due course I wafted back to the ground row to pluck the flowers which were usually lightly tacked. The incident is beautifully timed with the music: Giselle performs a *glissade,* a *temps levé* and a run, plucking first one flower and then the next. At this moment of purest Romantic poetry, I bent to take the flower, and the bloom remained firmly where it was. A quick extra pull revealed that they were nailed to the ground row, firmly battened down by the stage hands to avoid, so *they* thought, any sabotage. My usual "one and two" with the music was lost. The music was flying past. The lilies were still obstinately grounded. With no time for any pretty dallying, this ethereal spirit of Giselle gave one almighty wrench and then another, tearing the lilies from their moorings with superhuman—perhaps supernatural—strength. I caught up with the music within a couple of bars and managed to toss them, airborne, to my Albrecht.

With this final attempt by Fate to reduce the evening to shreds, matters improved. I am happy to record that the production was wonderfully well received, and that Lifar and I had a heart-stirring reception from the Met. audience. The Ballet Russe de Monte Carlo seemed to have "arrived", additionally so since the closing ballet of the evening was *Gaîté Parisienne* in which Choura and Massine were glorious.

As a postscript to this tense *Giselle* there is the more humorous incident which came when I was dancing with Ballet Theatre, and had been reunited with Pat Dolin as my Albrecht. We were in New York at the Met., and I was waiting in the wings to make my appearance through the door of Giselle's cottage. I heard the music for my entrance, and then the taps on the door which tell Giselle that Albrecht is calling for her. I went to open the door as usual. It refused to budge. I tried again, and with mounting panic heard the music continuing. The audience, of course, knew the ballet well, and they were waiting to welcome me in what is one of the best known first entrances in ballet. There seemed a terrible hush in the auditorium. The conductor, Robert Zeller, would now be dreadfully puzzled, and so would Pat. I started to shake the door. Not only the door but the whole of the cottage apparently started to tremble, and I could hear Pat's voice calling to me as he stood just around the side of the house, waiting in hiding for the appearance of his beloved Giselle. He whispered, "Stop shaking the house down, ducky! I'll come round and let you out!" By now I was in a state of panic, and I simply dared not wait. I backed out of the house into the wings, and decided to make my entrance down-stage, supposedly through Giselle's garden. As I dashed round to get on stage, Pat went off up-stage to come round into the cottage and free his Giselle from her temporary prison. But I was already down-stage, and came skipping on from the lower wing and reached centre stage. Musically I had now lost so much time that I did not have a clue where I was in the score. I can best describe my feelings as those of a little bull who comes into the corrida ring blazing with sunlight—dazzled and bewildered. I took the stage with no sense of direction, and to a dreadful silence in the auditorium. Mercifully the house broke into applause as people realized that all was well and that some delay must have kept me in the wings and away from the cottage. Pat now came bounding on to the stage from his quest for me in the wings, and by the beginning of the little mime-scene in which Giselle is so shy, we had managed to catch up with the music.

We danced the scene in a state of complete bewilderment, and as soon as I got off stage I asked the stage-manager for an explanation. All was soon revealed. A new stage-hand had seen the cottage door swing open just before curtain-rise, and had decided to put in a nail above the door and bend it down to make a small swivel that would allow the door to open when you turned the nail up. I had not been told of this innovation, and in my panic I had certainly not thought of looking up to see if there was some sort of catch—in every sense of the word! I had checked the door earlier, as I checked all the properties, before I went to dress for the performance, but the stage hand had gone to work after that. Thereafter, I always tested the door *just* before my entrance!

*Filming* Giselle *with Anton Dolin and Festival Ballet in 1951 at Riverside Studios. The camera-man is Terence Young; the director, Henry Caldwell. We filmed during the Stoll Theatre season in three days, and I used to rise at 5 a.m. to get to the studio, having danced* Giselle *at the theatre the night before.*

Giselle *Act One, Festival Ballet, Stoll Theatre, 1950.*

Giselle *Act Two with Ballet Theatre,*
*at the Palais de Chaillot, Paris, 1953.*
*The costume is by Eugene Berman.*

Giselle *Act One: the Mad Scene, with*
*the Sadler's Wells Ballet, Covent*
*Garden, 1957.*

Giselle *Act Two for BBC TV in 1955, top, with Erik Bruhn and Ballet Rambert. Left, with Marie Rambert and Erik Bruhn, and, opposite, with Erik Bruhn.*

The finale of Ruth Page's The Merry Widow, *Chicago, 1955. Decor and costumes were by Rolf Gérard. Opposite, the first scene and the theatre awning in New York, December 1955.*

*Coming and Going. The toy animals weren't mine, they were gifts for my nephew, Nigel.*

*I received the C.B.E. during the Italian Opera season at Drury Lane, when I was appearing in* The Pearl Fishers.

" You've got quite a long way to go before you'll be getting a C.B.E., dear ... "

*Above: Being presented to H.M. The Queen at the Royal Variety Performance in 1957.*

*Above left: Princess Margaret and Princess Anne at the Royal Academy of Dancing Gala matinée at the Coliseum, in November 1958. My colleague the great Spanish dancer, Antonio, is standing next to me.*

*Being presented to Princess Benedikte of Denmark at the Plaza Hotel, New York, May 6 1965, with Victor Borge.*

Renewing acquaintance with Liberace at the Café de Paris, London, 1951. I attended his very first performance in Chicago.

With James Starbuck during rehearsals for NBC's Show of Shows, New York, 1953.

*Rehearsing, accompanied by Tommy Steele, at the Royal Command Variety Performance at the Palladium in 1957.*

Sunday Night at the Palladium *on television in 1957. Being "partnered" by Tommy Trinder for the Snowflakes scene from* The Nutcracker.

*In my dressing-room in Paris, after dancing* Giselle *as a guest with Festival Ballet, at the Théâtre Sarah Bernhardt: with Charlie Chaplin and my sister Doris. Charlie Chaplin loved the ballet and had been an admirer of mine since my first performances in Hollywood with the Ballet Russe de Monte Carlo, which gave him the idea for* Limelight.

*With Bob Hope and Sir Laurence Olivier in a sketch we performed at* The Night of a Hundred Stars *at the Palladium in 1959.*

Bacchanal *with Milorad Miskovich in a BBC TV biographical film about Pavlova in 1956.*

*"Taglioni and the Scotsman", the opening scene of* La Sylphide *staged for Tyne Tees Television in 1960. The last time Anton Dolin and I danced together.*

Taglioni's ballet shoe. This shoe was sent to me by admirers in Dublin, who had heard of my performances as Taglioni in The Pas de Quatre, and remembered that Taglioni had stayed as a guest of their grandparents, and that their family still kept one of the great ballerina's shoes. This they sent to me—and it fits me perfectly.

# Manya

*In 1982 I donated many of my costumes, wigs, and my theatrical trunks, to the Theatre Museum in London as a gift to the nation.*
*With Alexander Schouvaloff, Director of the Theatre Museum, and Philip Dyer, consultant to the Museum.*

I OWE A GREAT DEAL TO MADAME MANYA.

She was a costumière of genius, who had made costumes for Pavlova, and travelled and lived with the great ballerina for many years until Pavlova's death in 1931. At that moment Manya declared that she would never again make costumes for any dancer. But in 1933 I received a note from her, saying that if I ever needed costumes, she would be happy to make for me. She became a true friend, making costumes for me, travelling with me, and also providing me with many off-stage clothes as well. She became like a member of my family, and looking at my stage costumes today I recall the infinite care she took in her work, and the immaculate skill she displayed. Manya was a real artist, inventive and imaginative in all the hand painting, cutting, spraying, dying she undertook. She was also a magician, taking away fabrics that I found and returning a week later with some astonishing creation for me to wear. Her work was unique in the perfection of its craft: no one could copy her, for her gift was wholly her own, though many people tried to emulate her.

At the Theatre Museum in London, the detail of her stitching—the inside of a costume as carefully and as lovingly made as the outside—fascinates connoisseurs and curators. Her skill is typified by the fact that the pearl-sewn and jewelled bodices to my costumes were always covered with the finest, almost invisible net, so that during a *pas de deux,* when a partner's hands must hold or lift me at the waist, no loose jewels or pearls ever fell off on to the stage.

It was Manya who invented the light-weight whalebone hoops in tutus, which she first made for Pavlova's use in the tropics so that humidity could not affect the tarlatans of the skirt and make it "droopy". Manya loved natural materials—silks, velvets—but with the advent of man-made fibres she grew to accept the new materials and her great talent showed her how to use them to the best advantage.

I treasured Manya as a devoted friend as well as a costume-maker. She made many of my costumes, starting with those for *Swan Lake* and *The Rake's Progress* at the Wells in the early 1930s, and everything that I wore with the Markova–Dolin Ballet. At the outbreak of war, when I went to America, contact was lost when both our homes were bombed. I was extremely happy to be reunited with her in 1948, when she resumed making all my costumes, which she continued doing until her death.

Her last creation for me was the Tyrolean dress I wore in the dances from *William Tell* in 1958.

L'Après-midi d'un faune. *My farewell performance—at London Festival Ballet's Birthday Gala in 1962.*

# SIXTY YEARS OF BALLET & OPERA

ONE OF THE MOST IMPORTANT THINGS I RECALL ABOUT DIAGHILEV was his great love of opera. We have to remember that the Russian Season in Paris in 1908 featured only opera and that dance came in tandem with opera in the 1909 Season, which brought Russian Ballet to the West. I always felt this love of opera when I was with the Diaghilev Ballet. Sometimes, later in my career, and often today, I have sensed a friction between opera and ballet, with ballet feeling it is being treated as the Cinderella of an opera house. But when I joined Diaghilev in 1925, we enjoyed and respected opera and it was an accepted fact that the company should do so. Operas featured in the Diaghilev seasons before I came to the company and, by the time I was a member, the Monte Carlo contract had been established between Diaghilev and the Principality, and short ballet seasons were followed by a longer stretch of opera performances. One of the reasons Diaghilev took the Monte Carlo contract was that extended opera seasons would allow time to prepare new ballets more easily, and for our repertory to be kept in order. During the opera seasons we had to be available to dance in the operas and also work on new ballets. It was an interesting way of life, because if we were not fortunate enough to be chosen to appear in the new ballets there was the compensation and pleasure of dancing in the operas, since there was a large operatic repertory.

I never felt that it was unrewarding, as do some dancers today, to dance in opera. The choreography was often very good—by Balanchine, no less—and the music was enormously satisfying. My first opera was the premiere of Maurice Ravel's *L'Enfant et les sortilèges,* which Balanchine choreographed, and in which I danced Smoke in the first part, and a Squirrel in the garden scene. How extraordinary it is to recall Ravel at the dress rehearsal, a slender, elegant, and to me, very handsome figure.

At this time the Monte Carlo Opera was very important because it stood as a half-way house between Paris and Milan. Singers did not jet around the world as they do today, and, en route from the Opéra to La Scala, they stopped off in Monte Carlo to give a few performances. I was fortunate as a young dancer to hear many of the greatest singers of the age, who came to our theatre for maybe just one production. I recall *Thaïs* with Fanny Heldy, who came on stage "topless" for the scene in which Thaïs must undress before the monk. In my second year with the company I appeared in *Thaïs* as a hand-maiden carrying flowers—and in Monte Carlo in the spring, an abundance of fresh flowers were thrown. The joy of this

*Previous page: Coaching Mary McKendry of London Festival Ballet in* Les Sylphides.

was that, after the performance, they were gathered up and we flower-maidens were allowed to take them home. I used to return to my mother at our *pension* with my arms full of headily fragrant carnations and mimosa. I should add that when Fanny Heldy actually stripped during the opera, Serge Grigoriev used to beckon me off-stage to the wings since he did not wish me to see the Diva topless.

The choreography for the operas was, as I have mentioned, provided by George Balanchine: this was what Diaghilev initially asked him to do, though George had never staged an operatic dance scene in his life. (Prior to this, Bronislava Nijinska had made very interesting dances.) Balanchine's opera ballets were fascinating because he used to try out intriguing choreographic ideas in them, and I later recognized some of these "experiments" in his ballets. In *Faust* I was cast as one of the angels who fly Marguerite to Heaven, and I was always grateful for the extra "danger money" I received for donning flying harness and taking to the air.

In the Monte Carlo company was John Brownlee, a gifted singer fresh from Australia who was then a young man. He was six years older than I, but we both seemed to count as the babies of our respective companies, and we first met at the Charity matinées and Tea Dances which were given in the afternoons in aid of the Monegasque Red Cross. I would be sent by Diaghilev to dance one of my solos—the Rubinstein *Valse Caprice* or the *Sylvia* pizzicato—and John would represent the opera with an aria or a ballad. It was felt that this gave both of us important experience with a not-too-demanding audience. Years later we met again at the Metropolitan Opera House in New York, and often broadcast together. Another opera friend was Maggie Teyte, whom I admired immensely. In New York she came to see several performances of Tudor's *Romeo and Juliet*, especially when Beecham was conducting, and it was she who suggested to Antony Tudor and me that *Pelléas* would make a fine balletic subject and that Mélisande would provide me with a beautiful new role.

Opera was very much part of our life with the Diaghilev Ballet—in the company's final season, at Covent Garden in the summer of 1929, we appeared first in the operas *Judith* and *Prince Igor* (where the Polovtsian Dances found their proper setting) before embarking upon the ballet programmes. I think we all loved and respected opera, and whenever we appeared— as often happened—in a major opera house, some of us would ask for house seats, or for passes, so that we could stand for performances of opera, or sit in the company box. I always took advantage of this privilege, and Serge Grigoriev was always pleased to let me see as much opera as I wanted. In Milan we were most fortunate when we appeared at La Scala. How well I remember Eva Turner as Turandot, and the blaze and splendour of her voice. We share a pioneering spirit for our country and for our art, and perhaps because of this we are friends to this day.

*Dame Eva Turner's 90th birthday party at the Royal Opera House, Covent Garden, in 1981, with Lord Miles, Dame Eva, Sir Michael Tippett, Sir Geraint Evans.*

My love for opera has continued throughout my career, and it became especially significant during the 1950s when I was invited to dance with the Metropolitan Opera in New York. The theatre had been a home for me since 1938 and the first Ballet Russe de Monte Carlo appearance there, and every year it seemed that I was to spend at least two seasons there. In 1953/54 I was invited to dance in *Die Fledermaus,* and I was subsequently to return for two seasons in Gluck's *Orfeo* with dear Papa Monteux conducting—and also celebrating his eightieth birthday. The Met., indeed, had been so much my home that I had a permanent dressing-room which I shared only with Kirsten Flagstad. When the "old" Met. was pulled down in 1966, all its interior furnishings, from the great gold curtain to what estate agents call "fixtures and fittings", were sold at auction, and an admirer bought me the door-knob from "my" dressing-room. It is a far from glamorous object, but I treasure it, recalling the various emotions that Flagstad and I felt, leaving the dressing-room, perhaps nervous and apprehensive to go on stage, and returning with great happiness after a performance, warmed by the joy of the audience.

*Receiving the Royal Academy of Dancing's Coronation Award in 1963 from Margot Fonteyn, who has always seemed like a younger sister to me.*

In January 1963, after I had announced my retirement, I was passing through New York en route for a much-needed holiday when I received a call from Rudolf Bing, General Manager of the Met., inviting me to the dress rehearsal of *La Sonnambula* in which many of my friends were appearing. I was asked if I would postpone my vacation in order to work with the dancers of the Met.'s Ballet company, who wanted me to stage the Rose Adagio from *The Sleeping Beauty* and the *Sylphides pas de deux* for them, as part of their Educational Programme. I was

*Working at the Metropolitan Opera House, New York. With Hans Brenaa; Antony Tudor; Audrey Keane, my ballet mistress; Irving Owen, our pianist; and Joseph Lazzini—for the Met. Ballet Evening in 1966. Directing the midnight rehearsal of the Metropolitan Opera Ballet for Macy's Thanksgiving Day float, New York, November 1964.*

*Choreographing the ballet for* Manon *in our studio at the old Met., with Ivan Allen.*

METROPOLITAN OPERA

NEW PRODUCTIONS
SEASON 1964-1965

GAETANO DONIZETTI

LUCIA DI LAMMERMOOR

CONDUCTOR: SILVIO VARVISO    STAGED BY MARGHERITA WALLMANN
SETS AND COSTUMES DESIGNED BY ATTILIO COLONELLO
CHOREOGRAPHY BY ALICIA MARKOVA
FIRST PERFORMANCE OCTOBER 12, 1964

CAMILLE SAINT-SAENS

SAMSON ET DALILA

CONDUCTOR: GEORGES PRÊTRE    STAGED BY NATHANIEL MERRILL
SETS AND COSTUMES DESIGNED BY ROBERT O'HEARN
CHOREOGRAPHY BY ZACHARY SOLOV
FIRST PERFORMANCE OCTOBER 17, 1964

RICHARD STRAUSS

SALOME

CONDUCTOR: KARL BÖHM    STAGED BY GUNTHER RENNERT
SETS AND COSTUMES DESIGNED BY RUDOLF HEINRICH
CHOREOGRAPHY BY ALICIA MARKOVA
FIRST PERFORMANCE FEBRUARY 3, 1965
BENEFIT · METROPOLITAN OPERA GUILD
KNABE PIANO USED EXCLUSIVELY

STUDIO
OF THE
METROPOLITAN
OPERA COMPANY
Dame Alicia Markova
DIRECTOR
FRIDAY
MAY 22
2:00 P.M.
Theatre Section
St. Paul Auditorium
SOLD OUT

happy to do this and (again, before I could get away), Rudolf Bing told me that the dancers had requested that I should assume the directorship of the Opera Ballet and be responsible for the dances and the "movement" in the operatic repertory. This was a fascinating challenge and thus my retirement lasted a mere three weeks before I found myself back in harness.

I returned briefly to London to organize my life, and to attend the investiture at Buckingham Palace where I received the honour of the D.B.E., and then made my way back to the Met. My arrival in New York was the occasion of a most terrifying experience. Two burglars were awaiting me in my hotel suite and I was held up, with a knife pointed at my stomach and a gun at my back. They had been ransacking my bedroom, and now they tied me up and flung me face down on my bed. The shock, and the fact that I was brutally trussed up, caused me to faint, and the burglars took fright and fled. Eventually I managed to knock my telephone off its hook, and call for help. The intruders, of course, escaped, and were never caught.

I was to spend six years with the Met. Ballet, three of them in the old house, and a further three in the transfer and installation of the company into the new Met. on Lincoln Center Plaza. These were busy years in which we initiated a series of independent ballet performances for my dancers. I also lectured and worked with the Educational Group, choreographed operas, and invited guest choreographers to work with the company. The independent ballet evenings included such *coups* as the first American staging of *Echoing of Trumpets* by Antony Tudor, then director of the Met. Ballet School, and the world première of his *Concerning Oracles,* and the presentation of a tremendous *Miraculous Mandarin* by Joseph Lazzini, with most innovative design by Bernard Daydé. My own stagings and choreographies included the necessary classical productions for my dancers, and I had the joy of working with many great conductors, producers and singers: an especial pleasure was a *Salome* produced by Gunther Rennert and conducted by Karl Böhn, with the magnificent Birgit Nilsson.

This happy and productive association ended on a sad note for me, for I sustained two serious falls in the new Met., and was to know operations, many months of pain, and a permanent incapacity to one knee. Then came a strike, and a protracted "lock-out" by the management, so that for nine months no work was possible in the house. I had during the Met. years become a lecturer, represented by Colston Leigh, travelling all

*With George Balanchine, New York, 1965, forty years after* Le Rossignol.

*In Monte Carlo, 1964, with Greer Garson, Pat Dolin and Milorad Miskovich.*

over America to give talks. My injury had prevented my fulfilling an engagement at the University of Cincinnati, and now, after a recuperative holiday, I was able in the spring of 1970 to go to Cincinnati to speak. While I was there, David McLean, director of the local Civic Ballet (a semi-professional company), asked me to stage Dolin's *Pas de Quatre* for his dancers. I was happy to do this, and within a couple of weeks I was asked if I would consider a University appointment as Distinguished Lecturer in Ballet. The chance to work with eager young dancers, to help guide them, to give lectures and to participate in the life of the University, with its handsome new buildings, was very attractive. I accepted, and a year later was nominated Professor, and continued working in Cincinnati for a further three years. Then, at the age of sixty-four, I felt the need to return to my national roots.

*With Mikhail Fokine's son, Vitale Fokine, at the dress rehearsal for the Metropolitan Opera Ballet at the Lewisohn Stadium. New York, 1965.*

*In Phoenix Arizona, relaxing with Vaslav Nijinsky's second daughter, Tamara, and a dear friend of many years, Terence Kennedy.*

In 1973 Arnold Haskell celebrated his
70th birthday, and Nadia Nerina and
her husband, Charles Gordon, organised
a wonderful reunion of Arnold's friends
and colleagues from around the world.
From left to right: Nadia Nerina,
Alicia Alonso, Ninette de Valois,
Arnold Haskell, Alicia Markova,
Yvette Chauviré, Galina Ulanova.

In New York in 1983 with Natalia
Makarova and Frederick Ashton,
after seeing Natasha in On Your
Toes.

*With the indomitable Lucia Chase, Director of American Ballet Theatre, and Leopold Stokowski, at a fund-raising luncheon in New York, 1963.*

*Souvenir of a dear friend, Ted Shawn, on his 80th birthday in New York: at the Dance Collection of New York Public Library, in 1971.*

In Houston, Texas, at the tribute gala for the Ballet Russe de Monte Carlo stars: on stage for the last time with Anton Dolin. What can I say about a unique friendship, on stage and off, that lasted for more than 60 years? We both retired from dancing, but our partnership continued until 1983 when we stood on stage for the last time in Houston. I feel our partnership existed because of our love, devotion and respect for each other and, above all, for the Dance.

*Opposite: Dolin's* The Pas de Quatre *in rehearsal in 1948. I am with Mia Slavenska, Alexandra Danilova, Natalie Krassovska, for the Ballet Russe de Monte Carlo.*

*At the reunion of the Ballet Russe de Monte Carlo stars. Back row: Ben Stevenson, director of the Houston Ballet; Leon Danielian; Frederic Franklin; Anton Dolin; Igor Youskevich; "Jeannot" Cerrone, who started with us in Monte Carlo in 1938 and is now General Manager of the Houston Ballet. Front row: Tatiana Semenova, of the Houston Ballet; Natalie Krassovska; Alicia Markova; Mia Slavenska; Irina Baronova.*

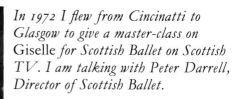

*In 1972 I flew from Cincinatti to Glasgow to give a master-class on* Giselle *for Scottish Ballet on Scottish TV. I am talking with Peter Darrell, Director of Scottish Ballet.*

*Coaching dancers of the Royal Ballet's* Ballet for All *in* Les Sylphides *in 1972.*

*Coaching young students at David Gayle's Yorkshire Ballet Seminars in 1980. For 12 years David Gayle has directed these admirable summer schools, the first residential ballet seminars in Britain.*

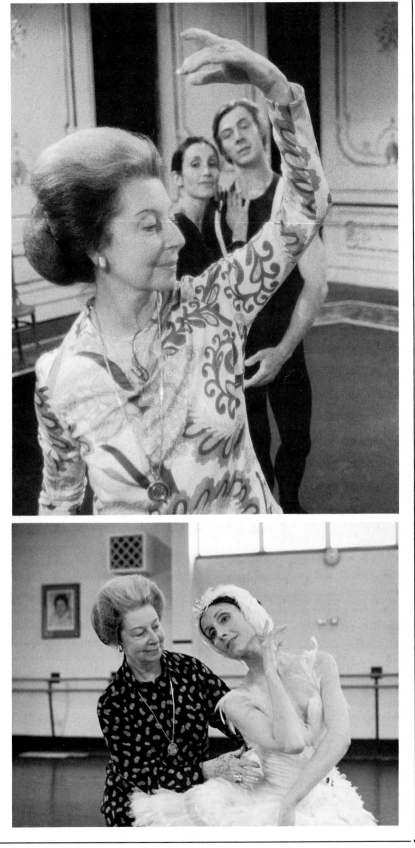

*In 1981 I gave a series of Master Classes on BBC TV in which I worked with Margaret Barbieri and David Ashmole of Sadler's Wells Royal Ballet.*

*Producing Margaret Barbieri of Sadler's Wells Royal Ballet in Fokine's* The Dying Swan.

*Taking a curtain call after the first night of my production of* Les Sylphides *for Northern Ballet Theatre at Sadler's Wells, July 1982.*

*H.M. The Queen meeting young American ballerina Katherine Healy at the Royal Celebration of Youth transmitted by Yorkshire TV, Harrogate, December 1985.*

*At the Anton Dolin Tribute Gala at the Royal Opera House, Covent Garden, in 1985, with my sisters Doris, Vivienne, and Berenice (Bunny).*

*On the last night of its season at Sadler's Wells Theatre, in November 1985, London Festival Ballet marked my 75th birthday with a performance, and a cake which was brought on stage at curtain fall. The company was celebrating its 35th year; I was also taken back more than 50 years to the days when I was dancing with the Vic-Wells Ballet on this same stage. In this curtain call, Peter Schaufuss, present director of London Festival Ballet, was joined by two distinguished predecessors, Beryl Grey and John Field. Behind me is my birthday cake.*

In 1974, after more than half a century of constant work, I hoped that I might find more time to spend with my family, and even find some time for myself. Twelve years later, I survey the years that have passed and wonder where they have gone. I have been as busy as ever, and as richly happy, producing for London Festival Ballet; serving as a Governor of The Royal Ballet; teaching at The Royal Ballet School; coaching and mounting productions in Canada, Australia, Britain; completing twelve years at David Gayle's annual Yorkshire Ballet Seminars; appearing on television; acting as President of the London Ballet Circle, the All-England Dance Competition and the Arts Educational Schools, and as Vice-President of the Royal Academy of Dancing; and occupied with a myriad other projects, which make me feel that I still have not retired as I announced I would twenty three years ago.

I do not now think I ever shall.